FIDEL CASTRO

FIDEL CASTRO

John J. Vail

1·101358
VA

CHELSEA HOUSE PUBLISHERS
NEW YORK
PHILADELPHIA

SENIOR EDITOR: William P. Hansen
PROJECT EDITOR: Marian W. Taylor
ASSOCIATE EDITOR: John Haney
EDITORIAL COORDINATOR: Karyn Gullen Browne
EDITORIAL STAFF: Maria Behan
            Pierre Hauser
            Perry Scott King
            Kathleen McDermott
            Howard Ratner
            Alma Rodriguez-Sokol
            Bert Yaeger
ART DIRECTOR: Susan Lusk
LAYOUT: Irene Friedman
ART ASSISTANTS: Noreen Lamb
            Carol McDougall
            Victoria Tomaselli
COVER ILLUSTRATION: Kye Carbone
PICTURE RESEARCH: Matthew Miller

Frontispiece courtesy of UPI/Bettmann Newsphotos

Revised Edition

  3 5 7 9 8 6 4

Library of Congress Cataloging in Publication Data

Vail, John J. FIDEL CASTRO.

(World leaders past & present)
Bibliography: p.
Includes index
1. Castro, Fidel, 1927–   . 2. Heads of state—Cuba—
Biography.
I. Title. II. Series.
F1788.22.C3V35   1986   972.91'064'0924 [B]   86-6853

ISBN 0-87754-566-9
    0-7910-0561-5 (pbk.)

Contents

John Adams
John Quincy Adams
Konrad Adenauer
Alexander the Great
Salvador Allende
Marc Antony
Corazon Aquino
Yasir Arafat
King Arthur
Hafez al-Assad
Kemal Atatürk
Attila
Clement Attlee
Augustus Caesar
Menachem Begin
David Ben-Gurion
Otto von Bismarck
Léon Blum
Simon Bolívar
Cesare Borgia
Willy Brandt
Leonid Brezhnev
Julius Caesar
John Calvin
Jimmy Carter
Fidel Castro
Catherine the Great
Charlemagne
Chiang Kai-Shek
Winston Churchill
Georges Clemenceau
Cleopatra
Constantine the Great
Hernán Cortés
Oliver Cromwell
Georges-Jacques Danton
Jefferson Davis
Moshe Dayan
Charles de Gaulle
Eamon De Valera
Eugene Debs
Deng Xiaoping
Benjamin Disraeli
Alexander Dubček
François & Jean-Claude Duvalier
Dwight Eisenhower
Eleanor of Aquitaine
Elizabeth I
Faisal
Ferdinand & Isabella
Francisco Franco
Benjamin Franklin

Frederick the Great
Indira Gandhi
Mohandas Gandhi
Giuseppe Garibaldi
Amin & Bashir Gemayel
Genghis Khan
William Gladstone
Mikhail Gorbachev
Ulysses S. Grant
Ernesto "Che" Guevara
Tenzin Gyatso
Alexander Hamilton
Dag Hammarskjöld
Henry VIII
Henry of Navarre
Paul von Hindenburg
Hirohito
Adolf Hitler
Ho Chi Minh
King Hussein
Ivan the Terrible
Andrew Jackson
James I
Wojciech Jaruzelski
Thomas Jefferson
Joan of Arc
Pope John XXIII
Pope John Paul II
Lyndon Johnson
Benito Juárez
John Kennedy
Robert Kennedy
Jomo Kenyatta
Ayatollah Khomeini
Nikita Khrushchev
Kim Il Sung
Martin Luther King, Jr.
Henry Kissinger
Kublai Khan
Lafayette
Robert E. Lee
Vladimir Lenin
Abraham Lincoln
David Lloyd George
Louis XIV
Martin Luther
Judas Maccabeus
James Madison
Nelson & Winnie Mandela
Mao Zedong
Ferdinand Marcos
George Marshall

Mary, Queen of Scots
Tomáš Masaryk
Golda Meir
Klemens von Metternich
James Monroe
Hosni Mubarak
Robert Mugabe
Benito Mussolini
Napoléon Bonaparte
Gamal Abdel Nasser
Jawaharlal Nehru
Nero
Nicholas II
Richard Nixon
Kwame Nkrumah
Daniel Ortega
Mohammed Reza Pahlavi
Thomas Paine
Charles Stewart Parnell
Pericles
Juan Perón
Peter the Great
Pol Pot
Muammar el-Qaddafi
Ronald Reagan
Cardinal Richelieu
Maximilien Robespierre
Eleanor Roosevelt
Franklin Roosevelt
Theodore Roosevelt
Anwar Sadat
Haile Selassie
Prince Sihanouk
Jan Smuts
Joseph Stalin
Sukarno
Sun Yat-sen
Tamerlane
Mother Teresa
Margaret Thatcher
Josip Broz Tito
Toussaint L'Ouverture
Leon Trotsky
Pierre Trudeau
Harry Truman
Queen Victoria
Lech Walesa
George Washington
Chaim Weizmann
Woodrow Wilson
Xerxes
Emiliano Zapata
Zhou Enlai

CHELSEA HOUSE PUBLISHERS

ON LEADERSHIP

Arthur M. Schlesinger, jr.

LEADERSHIP, it may be said, is really what makes the world go round. Love no doubt smooths the passage; but love is a private transaction between consenting adults. Leadership is a public transaction with history. The idea of leadership affirms the capacity of individuals to move, inspire, and mobilize masses of people so that they act together in pursuit of an end. Sometimes leadership serves good purposes, sometimes bad; but whether the end is benign or evil, great leaders are those men and women who leave their personal stamp on history.

Now, the very concept of leadership implies the proposition that individuals can make a difference. This proposition has never been universally accepted. From classical times to the present day, eminent thinkers have regarded individuals as no more than the agents and pawns of larger forces, whether the gods and goddesses of the ancient world or, in the modern era, race, class, nation, the dialectic, the will of the people, the spirit of the times, history itself. Against such forces, the individual dwindles into insignificance.

So contends the thesis of historical determinism. Tolstoy's great novel *War and Peace* offers a famous statement of the case. Why, Tolstoy asked, did millions of men in the Napoleonic Wars, denying their human feelings and their common sense, move back and forth across Europe slaughtering their fellows? "The war," Tolstoy answered, "was bound to happen simply because it was bound to happen." All prior history predetermined it. As for leaders, they, Tolstoy said, "are but the labels that serve to give a name to an end and, like labels, they have the least possible connection with the event." The greater the leader, "the more conspicuous the inevitability and the predestination of every act he commits." The leader, said Tolstoy, is "the slave of history."

Determinism takes many forms. Marxism is the determinism of class. Nazism the determinism of race. But the idea of men and women as the slaves of history runs athwart the deepest human instincts. Rigid determinism abolishes the idea of human freedom—

the assumption of free choice that underlies every move we make, every word we speak, every thought we think. It abolishes the idea of human responsibility, since it is manifestly unfair to reward or punish people for actions that are by definition beyond their control. No one can live consistently by any deterministic creed. The Marxist states prove this themselves by their extreme susceptibility to the cult of leadership.

More than that, history refutes the idea that individuals make no difference. In December 1931 a British politician crossing Park Avenue in New York City between 76th and 77th Streets around 10:30 P.M. looked in the wrong direction and was knocked down by an automobile—a moment, he later recalled, of a man aghast, a world aglare: "I do not understand why I was not broken like an eggshell or squashed like a gooseberry." Fourteen months later an American politician, sitting in an open car in Miami, Florida, was fired on by an assassin; the man beside him was hit. Those who believe that individuals make no difference to history might well ponder whether the next two decades would have been the same had Mario Constasino's car killed Winston Churchill in 1931 and Giuseppe Zangara's bullet killed Franklin Roosevelt in 1933. Suppose, in addition, that Adolf Hitler had been killed in the street fighting during the Munich *Putsch* of 1923 and that Lenin had died of typhus during World War I. What would the 20th century be like now?

For better or for worse, individuals do make a difference. "The notion that a people can run itself and its affairs anonymously," wrote the philosopher William James, "is now well known to be the silliest of absurdities. Mankind does nothing save through initiatives on the part of inventors, great or small, and imitation by the rest of us—these are the sole factors in human progress. Individuals of genius show the way, and set the patterns, which common people then adopt and follow."

Leadership, James suggests, means leadership in thought as well as in action. In the long run, leaders in thought may well make the greater difference to the world. But, as Woodrow Wilson once said, "Those only are leaders of men, in the general eye, who lead in action. . . . It is at their hands that new thought gets its translation into the crude language of deeds." Leaders in thought often invent in solitude and obscurity, leaving to later generations the tasks of imitation. Leaders in action—the leaders portrayed in this series—have to be effective in their own time.

And they cannot be effective by themselves. They must act in response to the rhythms of their age. Their genius must be adapted, in a phrase of William James's, "to the receptivities of the moment." Leaders are useless without followers. "There goes the mob," said the French politician hearing a clamor in the streets. "I am their leader. I must follow them." Great leaders turn the inchoate emotions of the mob to purposes of their own. They seize on the opportunities of their time, the hopes, fears, frustrations, crises, potentialities. They succeed when events have prepared the way for them, when the community is awaiting to be aroused, when they can provide the clarifying and organizing ideas. Leadership ignites the circuit between the individual and the mass and thereby alters history.

It may alter history for better or for worse. Leaders have been responsible for the most extravagant follies and most monstrous crimes that have beset suffering humanity. They have also been vital in such gains as humanity has made in individual freedom, religious and racial tolerance, social justice, and respect for human rights.

There is no sure way to tell in advance who is going to lead for good and who for evil. But a glance at the gallery of men and women in *World Leaders—Past and Present* suggests some useful tests.

One test is this: Do leaders lead by force or by persuasion? By command or by consent? Through most of history leadership was exercised by the divine right of authority. The duty of followers was to defer and to obey. "Theirs not to reason why / Theirs but to do and die." On occasion, as with the so-called enlightened despots of the 18th century in Europe, absolutist leadership was animated by humane purposes. More often, absolutism nourished the passion for domination, land, gold, and conquest and resulted in tyranny.

The great revolution of modern times has been the revolution of equality. The idea that all people should be equal in their legal condition has undermined the old structure of authority, hierarchy, and deference. The revolution of equality has had two contrary effects on the nature of leadership. For equality, as Alexis de Tocqueville pointed out in his great study *Democracy in America*, might mean equality in servitude as well as equality in freedom.

"I know of only two methods of establishing equality in the political world," Tocqueville wrote. "Rights must be given to every citizen, or none at all to anyone . . . save one, who is the master of all." There was no middle ground "between the sovereignty of all and the absolute power of one man." In his astonishing prediction of 20th-century totalitarian dictatorship, Tocqueville explained how the revolution of equality could lead to the *"Führerprinzip"* and more terrible absolutism than the world had ever known.

But when rights are given to every citizen and the sovereignty of all is established, the problem of leadership takes a new form, becomes more exacting than ever before. It is easy to issue commands and enforce them by the rope and the stake, the concentration camp and the *gulag.* It is much harder to use argument and achievement to overcome opposition and win consent. The Founding Fathers of the United States understood the difficulty. They believed that history had given them the opportunity to decide, as Alexander Hamilton wrote in the first Federalist Paper, whether men are indeed capable of basing government on "reflection and choice, or whether they are forever destined to depend . . . on accident and force."

Government by reflection and choice called for a new style of leadership and a new quality of followership. It required leaders to be responsive to popular concerns, and it required followers to be active and informed participants in the process. Democracy does not eliminate emotion from politics; sometimes it fosters demagoguery; but it is confident that, as the greatest of democratic leaders put it, you cannot fool all of the people all of the time. It measures leadership by results and retires those who overreach or falter or fail.

It is true that in the long run despots are measured by results too. But they can postpone the day of judgment, sometimes indefinitely, and in the meantime they can do infinite harm. It is also true that democracy is no guarantee of virtue and intelligence in government, for the voice of the people is not necessarily the voice of God. But democracy, by assuring the right of opposition, offers built-in resistance to the evils inherent in absolutism. As the theologian Reinhold Niebuhr summed it up, "Man's capacity for justice makes democracy possible, but man's inclination to injustice makes democracy necessary."

A second test for leadership is the end for which power is sought. When leaders have as their goal the supremacy of a master race or the promotion of totalitarian revolution or the acquisition and exploitation of colonies or the protection of greed and privilege or the preservation of personal power, it is likely that their leadership will do little to advance the cause of humanity. When their goal is the abolition of slavery, the liberation of women, the enlargement of opportunity for the poor and powerless, the extension of equal rights to racial minorities, the defense of the freedoms of expression and opposition, it is likely that their leadership will increase the sum of human liberty and welfare.

Leaders have done great harm to the world. They have also conferred great benefits. You will find both sorts in this series. Even "good" leaders must be regarded with a certain wariness. Leaders are not demigods; they put on their trousers one leg after another just like ordinary mortals. No leader is infallible, and every leader needs to be reminded of this at regular intervals. Irreverence irritates leaders but is their salvation. Unquestioning submission corrupts leaders and demeans followers. Making a cult of a leader is always a mistake. Fortunately hero worship generates its own antidote. "Every hero," said Emerson, "becomes a bore at last."

The signal benefit the great leaders confer is to embolden the rest of us to live according to our own best selves, to be active, insistent, and resolute in affirming our own sense of things. For great leaders attest to the reality of human freedom against the supposed inevitabilities of history. And they attest to the wisdom and power that may lie within the most unlikely of us, which is why Abraham Lincoln remains the supreme example of great leadership. A great leader, said Emerson, exhibits new possibilities to all humanity. "We feed on genius. . . . Great men exist that there may be greater men."

Great leaders, in short, justify themselves by emancipating and empowering their followers. So humanity struggles to master its destiny, remembering with Alexis de Tocqueville: "It is true that around every man a fatal circle is traced beyond which he cannot pass; but within the wide verge of that circle he is powerful and free; as it is with man, so with communities."

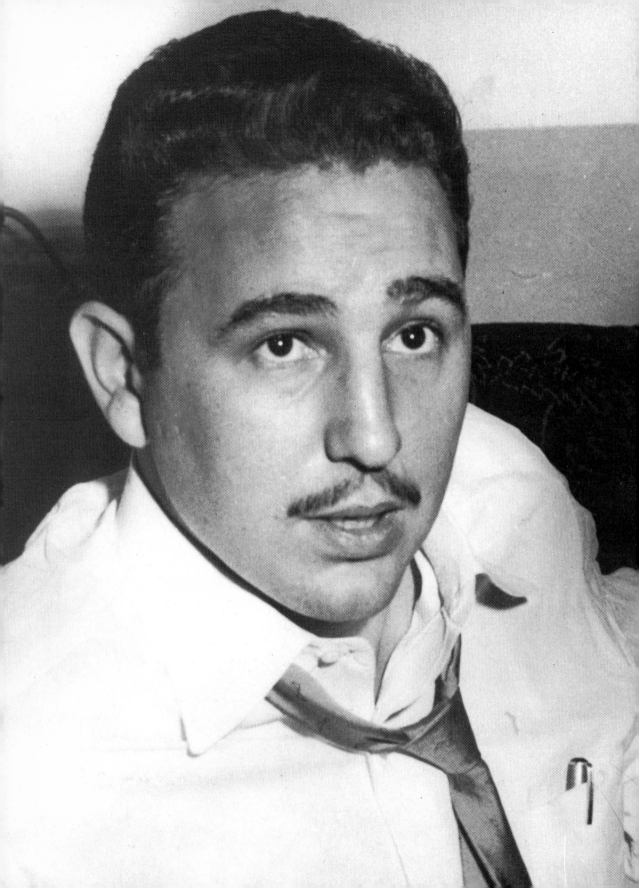

1

Birth of a Revolution

Pounded by cold rain and high winds, barely visible to each other in the chilly darkness, the men worked frantically to load their dangerous cargo. It was two o'clock in the morning on November 25, 1956. The men, who wore olive green uniforms, hurriedly stowed antitank guns, rifles, machine guns, pistols, ammunition, and supplies aboard the *Granma*, a 58-foot-long yacht moored in the harbor of Tuxpan, Mexico.

Because of the violent storm, the Mexican authorities had forbidden the departure of ships from the port. The *Granma*, however, slipped quietly out of Tuxpan and headed for the stormy open sea. The rain-soaked men on the deck talked in low voices about the chances of their aging, overloaded vessel staying afloat. Suddenly, their leader, a tall, intense man of 30, started to sing. The crew joined in, and spirits began to rise. The song was the national anthem of Cuba. The leader was Fidel Castro.

The 82 men aboard the *Granma* were about to start a revolution. They were headed for Oriente province, on the southeastern tip of Cuba. There, they planned to invade Cuba at the same moment

In October 1955, Cuban revolutionary Fidel Castro (b. 1926) announces the formation of his "26th of July Movement," aimed at toppling Cuban dictator Fulgencio Batista (1901–73). The movement — named for Castro's failed 1953 revolt against Batista — would accomplish its goal by the end of 1959.

THE BETTMANN ARCHIVE

Cuban poet and patriot José Martí (1853–95), whose memory Castro revered, was the hero of Cuba's 19th-century struggle for independence from Spain. "Anyone is a criminal," wrote Martí, "who promotes an avoidable war, and so is he who does not promote an inevitable civil war."

The motor yacht *Granma* lies peacefully at anchor off Cuba's Oriente province on December 5, 1956. Three days earlier, Castro and 81 other revolutionaries had disembarked from the yacht and waded ashore — marking the outset of the Cuban Revolution.

that a group of fellow revolutionaries staged an uprising in the Oriente city of Santiago de Cuba. They were counting on these moves to trigger a national revolt that would topple the regime of Cuba's hated dictator, Fulgencio Batista.

When the *Granma* left Tuxpan, she was more than 1,000 miles from her destination. Her top speed was only seven knots (about eight miles) per hour. Rocked by enormous waves and lashed by sheets of rain, she soon began to leak. The ship's rusted pumps no longer worked, and the men bailed feverishly until the storm ended at dawn. For three days the weather remained calm, but the sea grew rough again on November 30, the day the rebels had expected to land.

Off course and late because of the earlier storm, Castro and his men did not reach Cuba until December 2. By then, they learned from the radio aboard the *Granma* that the Santiago rebellion had been crushed by Batista's army. The *Granma* ran aground in shallow waters about 100 yards from the Cuban mainland. The exhausted men waded to shore through a thick swamp, leaving behind most of their weapons and supplies. When they reached firm ground hours later, they were cold, muddy, and bitterly disappointed by what seemed like the failure of their mission. They had no food and only a few weapons left. Their leader, Fidel Castro, nevertheless reassured his comrades. "Now," he said, "the days of the tyranny are numbered."

It may have seemed a deluded boast to proclaim that this group of shivering men was the liberation army promised the Cuban people. But only two

UPI/BETTMANN NEWSPHOTOS

years from that day, Fidel Castro would triumphantly lead his band of rebels into Havana at the
head of a victorious revolution.

Christopher Columbus, when he viewed the lush
Cuban shore on his first voyage to the New World
in 1492, had called it "the fairest island human eyes
have yet beheld," but the Caribbean paradise also
had a troubled and tempestuous history. Along with
Puerto Rico, Cuba had remained a Spanish colony
after most of the other Latin American countries
had fought for and won their independence early in
the 19th century.

Cuba's long struggle for independence began on
October 10, 1868. An army of liberation, consisting
of only 38 men, was formed by a 50-year-old plantation owner named Carlos Céspedes. Within two
days of the call for independence, the rebel army
had grown to 4,000 men; within a month, its ranks
had swelled to nearly 12,000. A freed black slave,
Antonio Maceo, became the rebels' military commander. A brilliant and daring tactician, Maceo
fought the Spanish soldiers to a standstill over a
10-year period, but he and his troops were unable
to dislodge the Spaniards from power.

On April 11, 1895, 61 years before Fidel Castro's
journey on the *Granma*, José Martí, a brilliant Cuban poet and patriot, landed in Oriente province
with a handful of men to continue the fight for independence. Killed in a battle with the Spanish a
month later, Martí became Cuba's national hero as

Smoke pours from the police
headquarters in Santiago,
Cuba, following a raid by
anti-Batista rebels on November 30, 1956. The Santiago uprising, scheduled to
coincide with Castro's invasion of Cuba, was crushed
by Batista's forces before
the delayed arrival of the
invaders.

 AP/WIDE WORLD PHOTOS

15

THE BETTMANN ARCHIVE

The American flag waves above the wreck of the *Maine* after a mysterious explosion ripped through the U.S. battleship in Havana harbor on February 15, 1898. The U.S. government, blaming Spain for the disaster, declared war on Spain on April 25, 1898. America won the war three months later.

Castro's parents, Lina Ruz González (d. 1953) and Angel Castro (d. 1956), in 1925. Angel, described by British historian Hugh Thomas as "reticent, violent, hard-working, and rich," was a self-made sugar magnate. His casual contempt for the law, says Thomas, may explain "his son's lack of interest in constitutionalism, bureaucracy, and formality of any kind."

16

the drive for freedom pressed onward.

The United States was both sympathetic to the rebels and interested in establishing its own influence in Cuba, which it saw as important to the defense of the Panama Canal. When an American warship, the *Maine*, exploded in Havana harbor in 1898, the United States blamed the Spanish, declared Cuba independent, and demanded Spain's withdrawal from the island. The United States was victorious in the three-month-long Spanish-American War that followed. Cuba became an independent nation in 1902, but the United States insisted on the new nation's agreeing to a plan known as the Platt Amendment. This legislation gave the United States the perpetual right to maintain military bases in Cuba, as well as the right to intervene in Cuba's affairs when it thought necessary. The Platt Amendment remained in force for 32 years, a period in which the United States frequently claimed its right to intervene.

Fidel Castro was born on August 13, 1926, on his father's sugar plantation near Birán, on the coast of Cuba's Oriente province. Fidel's father, Angel Castro, born in northwest Spain, had come to Cuba with the Spanish army during the Spanish-American War.

At the close of the war, Angel Castro decided to seek his fortune in Cuba rather than return to Spain. His first job was as a manual laborer for the U.S.-owned United Fruit Company. Angel was hardworking and shrewd, and by 1926, he had acquired

CUBAN COUNCIL OF STATE

CUBAN COUNCIL OF STATE

Fidel Castro — shown here at age three — grew up in a well-to-do family. While most of his schoolmates went barefoot and lived in hovels, the future revolutionary lived in a large, comfortable house, wore fine clothes, and always had plenty to eat.

more than 23,000 acres of sugarcane. His first marriage, to a Cuban schoolteacher, produced two children, Lidia and Pedro Emilio. Angel had a love affair with a Cuban peasant woman, who served as a cook in his household. After the death of his first wife, Angel Castro married the woman, Lina Ruz González, who had already borne him three children, Angela, Ramón and Fidel. After their marriage, the couple had three more daughters and a son, Raúl, who would become very close to his big brother Fidel.

Fidel led a carefree existence as a child. Tall and athletic, he spent his afternoons running or horseback riding through the fields of his father's huge farm with his brothers and sisters. Workers on the sugar plantation remember him as a wild, unruly youngster with tremendous drive. He enjoyed swimming with friends in a nearby river, but his great passion was the sea. Fidel eagerly anticipated his frequent visits to the harbor, where he would spend hours with the fishermen, listening spellbound as they told stories of struggles with sharks and whales.

Fidel's love of adventure was combined with a strong streak of rebelliousness. When he was about six, he demanded to go to school. Angel Castro saw little need for the schooling that neither he nor his wife had had. At first he refused Fidel's request, but the boy was so persistent that his father finally gave in and enrolled him in a local public school.

Fidel's schoolmates were the children of poor families of the area. They usually came to school barefoot and miserably clad. Fidel's experiences with them undoubtedly helped sensitize him to economic injustice and played a role in shaping his future political outlook.

In 1942, when he was 16, Fidel started high school in Havana. He attended the fashionable Belén Preparatory School, which was run by the Jesuits, an order of Roman Catholic priests. At Belén, one of the best secondary schools in Cuba, Fidel became a brilliant student, excellent debater, and champion athlete in baseball and track. (He was voted Cuba's best high school athlete in 1944.) The note under his photograph in the June 1945 graduating class yearbook said, "We do not doubt that he will fill the book of his life with brilliant pages."

In some respects, Fidel never lost his country-boy qualities. His indifference to clean clothes earned him a distinctive nickname: *Bola de Churre* ("Dirtball"). He preferred hikes with his friends to school dances, and he never quite mastered the social graces of his city-bred peers. Still, he was known for his relaxed charm, which made even his eccentricities stylish.

Fidel's rebellious nature was evident in high school. In his first year at Belén, he was challenged to a fistfight by an older and bigger student, who beat him until Fidel was no longer able to stand. The next day, Fidel, seeking to revenge his earlier humiliation, assailed his adversary and was beaten again until they were separated by bystanders. On the third day, they again fought to a standstill, but by now the other boy had had enough of fighting. "The most important feature of Fidel's character," said his brother Raúl years later, "is that he will not accept defeat."

Castro entered the University of Havana in 1945. A distinctive feature of Cuban university life was the violence of its student political activities: university elections were often settled by fists and guns. The university political scene was dominated by violent "action groups" that gave themselves such titles as the Socialist Revolutionary Movement or the Revolutionary Insurrectional Union.

In this volatile environment, politics became Castro's consuming passion. He decided to become a law student. Although he spent relatively little time on his studies, his exceptional memory enabled him to pass most of his courses with honors.

> *[Castro was] a power-hungry person, completely unprincipled, who would throw in his lot with any group he felt could help his political career.*
> —fellow law student

CUBAN COUNCIL OF STATE

Fidel (left) with his brothers Raúl (center; b.1931) and Ramón (b. 1926) in 1939, when the three were students at Santiago's Colegio Dolores, a school run by Jesuit priests. After he graduated from Dolores, Castro went to a prestigious Havana prep school, and then to the University of Havana, where he studied law.

19

Castro poses in November 1947 with the Bell of La Demajagua, whose tolling had proclaimed the commencement of Cuba's struggle for independence from Spain in 1868. Protesting corruption in the administration of Cuban President Ramón Grau San Martín (1887–1969), the young revolutionary and his colleagues had carried the bell through Havana in an open convertible.

Castro was not an ordinary freshman. His dynamic qualities were soon apparent to his fellow students, who elected him to the university organization Federatíon Estudiantil Universidad in his first year. There he quickly acquired a circle of supporters who admired his speaking skills and leadership qualities. Castro became involved in rallies and protests against government policies; like most politically active students of his era, he also participated in an "action group."

In 1947 a combination of Cuban political groups and university students organized an expedition to invade the neighboring Dominican Republic and overthrow its hated dictator, General Rafael Trujillo. Castro left school to cast his lot with the would-be rebels. They trained for three months on a desolate, mosquito-infested island off the Cuban coast. Just as the conspirators launched their small invasion fleet, Cuban police suddenly appeared to stop them. Castro escaped arrest by jumping ship and swimming to shore.

When he returned to college in the fall, Castro hatched a wild scheme to bring the Bell of La Demajagua, whose tolling had proclaimed the beginning of Cuba's War of Independence against Spain in 1868, to Havana. There, he hoped, the tolling of the bell would both symbolize the anniversary of the War of Independence and call attention to the corrupt administration of Cuba's current president, Ramón Grau San Martín.

Castro and his friends persuaded the officials in Manzanillo, the small town where the bell was kept, to let them take it. The students then made a triumphant tour of Havana, with the bell displayed in an open convertible. When the bell disappeared from the university a few days later, Castro made the first major speech of his career. In front of the student assembly, he denounced the government's duplicity in the bell's disappearance: "The coming years presage misery. People have lost faith; but woe to those who have killed that faith when the people become angry."

In 1948 Castro was one of a group of radical students who attended a Pan-American conference in

Bogotá, Colombia. The students, unofficially representing several Latin American countries, intended to stage a protest against foreign influence, or "colonialism," in their homelands. The clash between students and the international diplomats at the conference started quietly, but it turned to chaos when a popular Colombian politician was assassinated by a fanatic. The murder was followed by a riot in which several thousand people died.

In the violent confusion, no one knew exactly who was to blame for the riots, but Castro and his fellow student delegates were suspected of trying to start a communist revolution in Colombia. Castro was spirited out of the country on a cargo flight hastily arranged by the Cuban ambassador.

The events in Bogotá made a powerful impression on Castro. He would never forget this evidence of the extraordinary violence that lay just beneath the peaceful surface of Latin American society.

On his return from Bogotá, Castro settled into a more conventional life. In October 1948 he married Mirta Díaz Balart, a philosophy student at the university. Their son, Fidelito, was born the following year. In 1950 Castro graduated from law school and immediately joined a small Havana law firm. This quiet respite would be only a short one in the turbulent life of Fidel Castro.

Leftist demonstrators riot in Bogotá, Colombia, during a 1948 inter-American conference of foreign ministers. Castro, who had come to the conference to protest colonialism in the Americas, was suspected of helping the Colombian Communist party in its effort to turn the riot into a revolution.

2

"History Will Absolve Me"

astro's law office was located in the old section of Havana. His clients ranged from student protesters, to vegetable vendors charged with price fixing, to policemen accused of murdering a worker during an antigovernment demonstration. Castro's first love was still politics, and he devoted most of his energies to making his mark on Cuba's political scene.

Castro and his generation inherited a stormy political past. Cuba's independence began in 1902, when the United States withdrew its troops and Tomás Estrada Palma became Cuba's first president. Cuba was an independent republic in name only, however. Three times in the next 23 years the United States sent troops to quell revolts and insure Cuba's loyalty to American interests. For seven of those years, Cuba's government was directly ruled by American representatives. Thus, political parties were completely discredited, elections were a farce, and corruption became a basic part of Cuban political life.

In the 1920s a generation of Cubans who were

Always ready to confront authority, Castro argues with a Havana police officer during a student demonstration in November 1950, soon after his graduation from law school. Discussing his university career, Castro later said, "I ask myself why I studied law. I don't know. I attribute it partly to those who said, 'He talks a lot. He ought to be a lawyer.' "

CUBAN COUNCIL OF STATE

THE BETTMANN ARCHIVE

Gerardo Machado (1871–1939) was president of Cuba from 1925 until he was deposed by a popular revolution in 1933. The corruption, brutality, and antilabor authoritarianism that characterized his administration continued under his successors, which intensified the opposition of radicals like Castro.

born under Spanish colonialism and came of age in the early years of the republic began to promote a national identity among the Cuban people. José Martí's writings were avidly circulated and discussed for the first time. The spectacular examples of the 1910 Mexican revolution and the 1917 Russian revolution seemed to these young Cubans to prove the truth of Martí's argument: only a violent revolution could end Cuba's dependence on the United States and bring about a democratic society.

In August 1933 a wave of strikes and demonstrations swept the country. They were sparked both by widespread economic distress and resentment of the corrupt and tyrannical government of General Gerardo Machado. Machado, who had been president since 1925, was driven from office.

At this point, a group of young noncommissioned officers, led by a sergeant named Fulgencio Batista, seized control of the army and overthrew Machado's successor. In 1934 the United States cancelled the Platt Amendment, making Cuba politically independent. (The United States, however, retained its naval base at Guantánamo Bay; the base continues to be American-occupied to this day.) Civilian and military presidents came and went over the next seven years, but the "strong man" behind Cuba's government was Batista.

During this period social and labor unrest increased in both the cities and the countryside. A nationwide strike was ruthlessly crushed in 1935. The nation's young radicals, now convinced that the 1933 revolution had been betrayed, became even more fixed in their desire for a complete reform of the government.

Meanwhile, Batista decided he wanted to be president in name as well as practice. He directed the writing of a new constitution for Cuba, a document that contained surprisingly liberal provisions about labor and social relations. Batista, elected in 1940, served as president for four years. Although his administration was relatively democratic, it was marked by serious corruption.

Throughout Cuba's cities, Batista and his handpicked police force organized an extensive system

> *Anyone is a criminal who promotes an avoidable war; and so is he who does not promote an inevitable civil war.*
> —JOSÉ MARTÍ
> 19th-century Cuban patriot

24

of extortion and kickbacks. All stores, bars, and commercial establishments were forced to contribute regularly to the local police precincts, which were also heavily involved in prostitution, gambling, and drugs.

In 1944 Batista, forbidden by the new constitution to hold the presidential office for consecutive terms, agreed to free elections. Dr. Ramón Grau San Martín, head of the Auténtico party, was elected. Batista left the country and took up temporary residence in Miami, Florida.

Grau's administration, while active in improving education and public health, nevertheless proved as corrupt as Batista's. Grau's successor was Carlos Prío Socarrás, also a member of the Auténtico party and also deeply involved in the corruption that infected every part of Cuban society. He served as president from 1948 to 1952.

The highly dishonest Auténtico administrations aroused disgust among many of the party's members. In 1947 a group of these disillusioned Auténticos had formed a new party, known as Ortodoxo.

Celebrating the overthrow of President Machado in August 1933, Cubans destroy furniture taken from Havana's presidential palace. Machado's successor, Manuel de Céspedes (1871–1939), governed Cuba for only a few weeks; he was deposed by Batista in September 1933.

Eduardo Chibás, the Ortodoxos' founder, was a charismatic politician committed to the legal route to power. He believed the Ortodoxos to be the true heirs to Cuba's revolutionary heritage. Fidel Castro, who was impressed by Chibás's ideas, joined the Ortodoxo party and helped Chibás campaign across the country. By 1951, Chibás had become the most popular politician in Cuba. His election to the presidency the following year was widely expected. That summer, however, Chibás committed suicide. His death shocked Cubans, especially Castro and his fellow Ortodoxos, but the party continued to grow.

Young Cubans' hopes and dreams of creating an honest and democratic society were dashed in early 1952. On March 10, three weeks before the scheduled presidential elections, Batista overthrew the constitutional government of Carlos Prío Socarrás. Aided by junior army officers, Batista carried out the coup swiftly and with little bloodshed. The officers seized the military garrison in Havana, leaving Prío Socarrás no choice but to flee the country.

Batista's motives for the military coup were simple. A legal candidate for the presidency himself, he knew he had no chance of winning the presidential elections; he was estimated to be running third to Auténtico and Ortodoxo candidates. Batista and his followers feared being displaced economically by the emergence of commercial interests controlled by rival groups. The coup insured Batista's continued grip on the government, which in turn guaranteed his continued profits from political corruption and gangsterism.

As Ramón Bonachea wrote in *The Cuban Insurrection:* "From a corrupt democracy, Cuba now shifted to a corrupt dictatorship." Batista immediately suspended all constitutional guarantees: elections were banned, freedom of speech and the press were heavily curtailed, and activities of the opposition parties were restricted. The United States officially recognized the Batista government 17 days after the coup, and Cuba's labor and business leaders quickly demonstrated their own support of the new regime. The opposition parties were in complete disarray due to ineffective leadership

The combatants of Moncada did not achieve their military objectives, but they did achieve their revolutionary objectives.
—FAUSTINO PÉREZ
Moncada rebel

and police repression. The only hint of meaningful opposition to the coup came from Cuba's students.

Fidel Castro was, of course, at the center of the protests. Three days after the coup, he issued a manifesto urging "courageous Cubans to sacrifice and fight back." The document concluded with the last two lines of the Cuban national anthem: "to live in chains is to live in shame; to die for the Fatherland is to live." A few days later, Castro requested Havana's court of appeals to punish those involved in the coup; his case was immediately dismissed by the court.

Batista's regime became increasingly corrupt, dictatorial, and brutal. Arrest, imprisonment without trial, and torture became commonplace. As their attempts to find peaceful and legal means to restore constitutional government repeatedly failed, Castro and other Cuban radicals decided their only choice was armed struggle. Advocates of violent action were everywhere, and Castro found many other young people who shared his feelings about Cuba's predicament. In May 1952 he told a group of sympathetic students and workers in Havana that a revolt was necessary. "Revolution," he said, "opens the way to true merit to those who have sincere courage and ideas, to those who risk their lives and take the battle standard in their hands." He said it was their duty to liberate Cuba: the task could not wait for another generation.

At first, Castro hoped to organize action groups among members of the Ortodoxo party who were willing to fight against Batista. He quickly realized, however, that few party members had the ability or the determination to overthrow the government. He decided to develop a new revolutionary strategy on his own. His plan was to attack the Moncada military garrison, near the city of Santiago in Oriente province. He hoped to capture an arsenal from which to arm his revolutionary followers. He also hoped the raid would inspire a popular uprising in Oriente, to be followed by a nationwide revolution. Such tactics were far from unprecedented; the idea of a small, well-organized minority attempting a bold military strike was firmly rooted in Cuba's rev-

UPI/BETTMANN NEWSPHOTOS

Batista acknowledges the cheers of supporters during a speech broadcast from the Cuban army's Camp Columbia barracks on September 4, 1934. The event marked the first anniversary of Batista's coup against the Céspedes government.

olutionary past.

Castro's followers, who became known as Fidelistas, were primarily men — and a few women — from the lower-middle class and the working class. Many had worked in factories or on large sugar plantations; the group even included two cooks from Belén, Castro's former school. Political militants since the 1933 struggle, the two had followed Castro's career for years and were anxious to be part of his movement.

The Fidelistas purchased a farm outside Santiago and raised $18,000 to buy arms and supplies. Many of them had sold their shops or donated their life savings in order to finance the attack. The group drew most of its ideas from the writings of José

As the Batista government celebrated its first year in office, Havana students burned an effigy labeled "I am Batista, the killer." Castro called the increasingly powerful leader "a representative of the military caste, of the corrupt politicians, of the big businessmen, of the great landowners, and of the foreign companies."

CUBAN COUNCIL OF STATE

Backed by a Cuban flag and a portrait of Eduardo Chibás (1907–51), Castro addresses a Havana meeting of the Ortodoxo party in 1951. The party was formed in 1947 by Chibás and other members of the Auténtico party who were disgusted with the corruption of its leader, Carlos Prío Socarrás (b. 1903).

Martí, and from the tradition of Cuba's revolutionary uprisings. Hugh Thomas states in his book, *The Cuban Revolution*: "Castro embarked on the Moncada attack without indeed a very carefully worked-out ideology, only a desire to overthrow the 'tyrant' Batista and also move on to destroy the whole rotten society . . . of old Cuba."

On July 25, 1953, the revolutionaries at the farm outside Santiago listened as Castro outlined his strategy for the attack. It would begin the next day at 5:30 A.M. Santiago was celebrating its annual carnival, and Castro counted on many of Moncada's soldiers attending the late-night festivities. This might leave them less ready to fight at dawn. Castro, with 79 men, would storm the barracks and attempt to capture the weapons armory. Raúl Castro, with

10 men, would seize the Palace of Justice, from whose roof he could provide covering fire for his brother's attack. The force's deputy commander, Abel Santamaría, would occupy the nearby hospital to treat the wounded. If the immediate objective failed, the rebels would retire to the mountains to begin a guerrilla war against the regime. Although his men were outnumbered ten to one (the barracks held close to 1,000 soldiers), Castro counted on the enemy's surprise and confusion to even the odds.

The night of July 25 was a tense one for the rebels. Somehow, the moon seemed brighter, the stars bigger, than ever before. The men searched the faces of their friends, faces they might never see again. They knew tomorrow they might change Cuba's history forever. "In the next few hours," Castro told them, "we shall win or we shall be defeated, but in either case, this movement will triumph. If we win this morning, it will hasten that to which Martí aspired. If we don't, the gesture will have set an example to the people of Cuba."

At 5:30 A.M. 26 carloads of men — rebels dressed as soldiers — arrived in Santiago. Raúl Castro and Santamaría easily captured the palace and hospital. The first rebels to pull up in front of the barracks shouted, "Make way for the general!" The sentries, bewildered by the ruse, were quickly disarmed. Just as Castro arrived, however, three machine-gun-equipped soldiers blocked his way. He struck two with his car, but the third escaped to sound the alarm. At the same time, the men following Castro, interpreting his action as the signal to attack, left their cars and opened fire on the barracks.

The rebels had lost the advantage of surprise. The soldiers in the barracks, now thoroughly awakened, opened up with a deadly hail of machine gun fire. Realizing the tide had turned, Castro gave the order to retreat. He and Raúl and their men withdrew, but the rebels at the hospital were surrounded. Abel Santamaría insisted on continuing to fight, thus giving Castro time to escape. "Fidel," he said to a companion, "is the one who must not die!"

Although only three rebels died in the attack, 80 were captured. Most of those prisoners, including

Marching towards an ideal
Knowing very well we are
*   going to win;*
More than peace and
*   prosperity*
We will all fight for liberty.
    —AGUSTÍN DÍAZ CARTAYA
        Cuban composer,
        from "The Hymn of
        the 26th of July"

Abel Santamaría, were tortured and subsequently executed. Although Batista claimed to be displeased by his soldiers' brutal treatment of the captured rebels, he approved the later executions, which set an example to other would-be revolutionaries. If the second largest garrison in Cuba had been open to attack, who knew what could happen next? In the aftermath of the failed raid, thousands of people were ruthlessly detained and questioned. Anyone wounded, even from an innocent accident, was in danger of interrogation and torture.

After the battle, Castro and his remaining men separated into groups and began their journey to the mountains. On the evening of August 1, 1953, a patrol under the command of Lieutenant Pedro Sarriá found and captured Castro and two companions in the house of a peasant sympathetic to the revolutionaries' cause. Learning of the rebel leader's capture, the Moncada garrison — which was under orders to kill Castro on sight — dispatched 20 soldiers to take charge of the prisoners. Lieutenant Sarriá, a compassionate officer who had already prevented the execution of two rebels, insisted that Castro be placed in the safety of a civil prison rather than be taken to Moncada. Sarriá's courage saved Castro's life. By the time Castro was handed over to the authorities in Santiago, it was too late for any more executions. Public opinion had been outraged by the savagery of the government troops at Moncada, and a number of Santiago notables, including the bishop and the chief justice, made themselves responsible for Castro's humane treatment.

The attack on Moncada was a military defeat, but, as Castro had predicted, it turned out to be an important political victory. Castro and his followers became the idols of a new generation of Cubans dedicated to changing Cuban society. As Celia Sánchez, Castro's secretary, wrote, "Moncada was the commencement of the struggle . . . it was the mother of the revolution."

Castro was kept in solitary confinement in a Santiago jail. The other Moncada prisoners were tried in September, but Castro was given a special secret trial on October 16, 1953. Although six reporters

Batista addresses troops at Camp Columbia in September 1952, six months after he had declared himself president of Cuba. Castro later said, "when none of the [Ortodoxo] leaders showed that they had the ability, the resolution, the seriousness of purpose to overthrow Batista, . . . I finally worked out a strategy on my own."

Castro (at left) and fellow revolutionaries in police headquarters in Santiago on August 1, 1953. Six days earlier, the rebels had failed in their attempt to capture the Moncada barracks in Oriente province. Tried two months later, Castro received a 15-year prison sentence.

and two attorneys were permitted to observe the proceedings, nationwide censorship was imposed and little news of the trial's events leaked out. Castro's two-hour speech in his defense later became the text of his famous manifesto, "History Will Absolve Me." His words have since become as famous to Cuban schoolchildren as Abraham Lincoln's Gettysburg Address is to American youth. In his closing statement, Castro said: "As for me, I know that imprisonment will be . . . filled with threats, ruin and cowardly deeds of rage, but I do not fear it, as I do not fear the fury of the wretched tyrant who snuffed out the lives of 70 brothers of mine. Condemn me. It does not matter. History will absolve me." Castro received a 15-year sentence. His brother Raúl got 13 years, and the other defendants received lesser terms.

Castro was imprisoned on the secluded Isle of Pines. Prisoners were allowed to exercise, send letters, and keep books in their cells. Castro spent most of his time reading novels by Hugo, Tolstoy, and Dostoevsky, or works on philosophy by John Locke and Thomas Aquinas. While he was in prison, Castro learned that his wife had accepted a job on the Batista payroll. The couple's relationship had become strained over the years due to Castro's absences and political fervor, but Mirta's implied support of the Batista regime through her employment led to a final breakup. The Castros were divorced in December 1954. Batista, meanwhile, was feeling increasingly confident. His regime maintained a warm relationship with the United States, the Cuban sugar business was booming, and antigovernment activities had decreased sharply. Batista was reelected president in November 1954, and the following spring he announced an amnesty (pardon) for all political prisoners.

Castro, along with Raúl and 18 other Moncada participants, was released from prison on May 15, 1955. On the ferryboat leaving the Isle of Pines, the group decided to continue their struggle together as the "26th of July Movement." Castro immediately immersed himself in opposition activities. He wrote newspaper articles attacking the regime, and spoke at several demonstrations. To his disgust, Castro found the opposition parties severely divided and squabbling among themselves about the best way to defeat Batista. His personal life was also cause for concern: his law practice was nonexistent, he was watched constantly by the police, and he feared assassination by Batista's agents. He decided that, for the moment, his options in Cuba were closed.

Like Martí before him, Castro was determined to carry out an invasion of Cuba from foreign soil. As he left for Mexico on July 7, 1955, he vowed to return the following year in triumph: "As a follower of Martí, I think that the hour has come to take one's rights, not to ask for them; to seize them, not to beg for them. From such voyages, either one does not return, or one returns with the beheaded tyranny at one's feet."

Prisoner No. 4914 — Fidel Castro — as he looked on beginning his 15-year sentence at Cuba's top-security Isle of Pines prison in October 1953. Released less than two years later, Castro soon departed for Mexico, where he began to organize a revolutionary army of Cuban exiles.

3

Guerrilla Chief

Seventeen months were to pass before Fidel Castro's fateful return to Cuba. Life in Mexico was difficult. The Cubans had almost no money, were continually harassed by the Mexican authorities, and lived under the ever-present threat of expulsion from the country. Hoping to improve the group's financial position, Castro embarked on a fund-raising trip to the United States — after borrowing money for his train fare. He spent seven weeks in the United States, visiting Cuban emigrés in New York, Philadelphia, and Miami, holding meetings and making speeches. He managed to raise several thousand dollars for his cause. Castro and the other men, however, continued to live from hand to mouth. Castro even had to pawn his coat to pay for the printing of the manifesto announcing the formation of the 26th of July Movement.

By March 1956, preparations for the invasion were under way. The men bought weapons, and during the day, a Cuban veteran of the Spanish Civil War taught them how to clean and reassemble guns and how to make bombs and Molotov cocktails (fire bombs). In the evenings, the men studied the man-

UPI/BETTMANN NEWSPHOTOS

Batista inspects a gun captured during Castro's unsuccessful July 26, 1953, raid on the Moncada barracks. As the revolutionary movement grew stronger, Batista ordered the suppression of all news of Castro's campaign in the Sierra Maestra.

Cradling his ever-present rifle, Castro is flanked by his brother Raúl (far left) and another armed follower at the rebel group's mountain hideout in southern Cuba's Sierra Maestra. By this time — September 1957 — the rebels had won several notable victories over Batista's forces and had gained the trust and respect of many of the local peasants.

Seemingly unperturbed by their arrest on charges of plotting against Batista, Castro (arrow) and 21 followers pose outside a Mexico City government building on June 24, 1956. When the rebels were released the next month, they continued their training in a variety of secret locations.

The plans he revealed seemed beyond his reach and I felt a kind of pity for this aspiring deliverer who was so full of confidence and firm conviction, and I was moved by his innocence.

—TERESA CASUSO
fellow Cuban exile in
Mexico with Castro

ifesto of the 26th of July Movement and the works of José Martí.

After a month's training in Mexico City, the rebels moved to a ranch outside the city. There, they embarked on 15-hour marches with full packs, crossing rivers, climbing mountains, and spending their nights on the ground. They learned and rehearsed guerrilla warfare: how to harass and confuse the enemy, how to retreat when pressured, how to ambush when certain of success.

Among the trainees were two men destined to play a leading role in the Cuban revolution. Ernesto Guevara, an Argentine doctor nicknamed "Che," had met Fidel Castro in July 1955, and been deeply impressed by Castro's unshakable faith and his willingness to risk death for his cause. Guevara came from an upper-class family, and could have easily lived a comfortable life, but like Castro, he chose revolution instead. Camilo Cienfuegos had been working in a restaurant in California when he read about Castro's pledge to invade Cuba. He quit his job and arrived in Mexico a short time before the rebels departed.

Meanwhile, some of the opposition leaders in Havana still hoped a compromise could be reached with the regime in power. They formally requested Batista to agree to free and open elections; their demands were flatly rejected. From Mexico City, Castro accused the opposition leaders of hypocrisy. Only months before, he pointed out, they had agreed that violent action was their only recourse against Batista. He wrote: "The Cuban people want more than a change of leaders. Cuba wants a radical change in its entire public and social life."

Castro's militancy was attracting a growing number of supporters in Cuba. Cries supporting the 26th of July Movement were heard at every political rally, and the number 26 was found painted on walls across the country. Ramón Bonachea, in *The Cuban Insurrection*, describes the occasion when the national baseball championship in Havana was interrupted by students who rushed onto the field carrying banners reading *"Abajo Batista!"* ("Down with Batista!"). Police savagely beat the unarmed youths in the middle of the baseball field as thousands of Cubans watched in horror on television. The protests had coincided with a nationwide strike of more than half a million sugar workers. Deep unrest was stirring in Batista's Cuba.

In November 1956 Castro received $40,000 from Prío Socarrás, the sympathetic Cuban opposition leader and ex-president. The money was used to buy the weather-beaten yacht *Granma*. A few weeks later, Mexican authorities, in collaboration with Batista's secret police, raided Castro's headquarters, confiscating arms and arresting more than 25 men.

A noble, generous, and valiant people who love peace cannot at any moment or under any circumstances give their backing to any infamous delinquent who places a bomb.
—from an editorial in *Información*, a Cuban newspaper, attacking terrorist activities by the 26th of July Movement

Cuban troops prepare to engage Castro's forces in the Sierra Maestra in December 1957. By now, the rebels had also established themselves in the Sierra Cristal — a mountainous region west of the Sierra Maestra — and were building up an elaborate network of communications centers and supply depots.

The Sierra Maestra, where Castro concentrated his operations from November 1956 until his troops captured El Uvero in May 1957. After the fall of El Uvero, the Cuban army's most important stronghold in the area, Batista withdrew all his forces from the Sierra Maestra.

Fearing continued police attacks, Castro decided to advance the invasion date. On the stormy night of November 25, Castro and his men crowded onto the *Granma* and began their journey towards Cuba.

Castro said, in a 1966 speech, "In truth, we can affirm that our revolution began under incredible conditions." On December 2 the *Granma* landed, several miles off course, in Oriente province. The November 30 uprising by the 26th of July Movement in Santiago had been crushed, and the military had been alerted about Castro's impending arrival. Realizing that they had been spotted by a government airplane as they waded ashore, Castro and his men quickly moved inland, abandoning most of their remaining supplies on the beach.

The rebels marched without food or water for three days. On December 5, unaware that a local farmer had betrayed them to government troops, the exhausted men stopped to rest in a sugarcane field. The field was surrounded by soldiers, who opened fire on the rebels. At least 20 of Castro's men were killed in the ambush; several surrendered and were shot, a few were captured and held for trial, and the rest fled in small groups. With two of his surviving men, Castro hid from the government soldiers for several days. They then began the hazardous journey to the safety of the mountains, the Sierra Maestra. Traveling only at night, they rested and hid during the day, eating nothing but the sugar they sucked from the ripening canes. Government planes circled continually, their loudspeakers booming demands for the rebels' surrender.

On December 17 Castro and his two companions reached the isolated farmhouse of Ramón Pérez, a peasant whose brother had joined the 26th of July Movement several months before. During the succeeding days, surviving members of the *Granma* expedition, including Raúl Castro, Che Guevara, and Camilo Cienfuegos, straggled in and were met with warm embraces. Their desperation soon gave way to a renewed conviction that they would succeed. Although only 17 of the original 82 rebels had made it to the Sierra Maestra, Castro spoke of vic-

Castro with his senior commanders in the Sierra Maestra in June 1957. Standing, second from the left, is Ernesto "Che" Guevara (1928–67). Guevara, an Argentinian physician, became a revolutionary in 1954, when Guatemala's socialist government was overthrown by right-wing, U.S.-backed army officers.

Castro's forces stepped up their activities in 1958. On just one day — February 26 — they raided a bank in Havana, burned a sugarcane field in Pinar del Río province, attacked a government patrol in Manzanillo, burned an American sugar mill near Guantánamo, and hurled grenades at Cuban army troops in Santiago de Cuba.

tory: "We are in the Sierras," he said. "The days of the dictatorship are numbered."

On Christmas Day 1956 the rebels set out to establish a base camp on Turquino Peak, at 8,600 feet, Cuba's highest mountain. Castro and his men knew only a few peasants and lacked knowledge of their surroundings.

The rebels were now in the roughest, wildest, and poorest area in Cuba. Its residents, who were largely illiterate, lived in tiny wooden shacks with earth floors. Indoor plumbing was unheard of, and electricity almost nonexistent. Suspicious at first, the peasants slowly began to trust the strangers. They sold them supplies and told them where they could find water and other necessities.

Meanwhile, Batista announced that the rebels had been wiped out. Castro was determined to prove him wrong. On January 15, 1957, the guerrilla army made its way to La Plata, an isolated army post. Under cover of darkness, the rebels opened fire from several directions and then stormed the barracks. After an hour of intensive fighting, the soldiers surrendered; two were killed, five wounded, and three captured. The guerrillas seized 12 rifles, one machine gun and over 1,000 rounds of precious ammunition. Several rebels suggested executing the captured soldiers, but Castro ordered them released unharmed. He said that this would teach the government troops that they could save their lives simply by surrendering. The guerrillas' humane treatment stood in direct contrast to the practice of Batista's troops, who with few exceptions, tortured and killed any rebel they took prisoner. "Only cowards and thugs murder an enemy when he has surrendered," said Castro. "The rebel army cannot carry out the same tactics as the tyranny which we fight."

La Plata marked the rebels' first military victory, but no news of the surprise attack leaked through the Batista censorship. Castro still needed to show the country that the guerrillas were alive and fighting in the Sierra Maestra. On February 17 a member of the 26th of July Movement guided Herbert Matthews, a correspondent for *The New York Times*, to Castro's mountaintop camp. In danger of being discovered during the interview by passing patrols, Castro and Matthews spoke in whispers.

Castro talked about the importance of carrying on the nationalist, anticolonialist tradition of José Martí. He told Matthews, "We have no animosity toward the United States and the American people. We are fighting for a democratic Cuba and an end to the dictatorship." Castro pledged that democratic freedoms would be restored and elections held, but he spoke only in vague terms of how he would accomplish the programs he promised.

Matthews's interview with Castro appeared the following Sunday as a lead story in the *Times*, with a photograph of the revolutionary holding his rifle. The article turned Castro into an international figure and presented him as the heart of Cuba's resistance to Batista. Most important, it escaped Batista's censorship, and gave definite proof that the guerrillas were active under the leadership of Fidel Castro.

Despite the attention they now received, fighting

The attack on the small barracks at the mouth of the La Plata river in the Sierra Maestra brought us our first victory, and had repercussions which reached beyond the craggy region where it took place. It came to everyone's attention, proving that the rebel army existed and was ready to fight.
—ERNESTO "CHE" GUEVARA
Argentine-born Cuban
revolutionary

CUBAN COUNCIL OF STATE

Castro instructs new recruits Celia Sánchez (right; 1923–80) and Haydée Santamaria (1927–80) in the use of semiautomatic weapons in May 1957. Sánchez, the daughter of a wealthy dentist, later became Castro's secretary; Santamaria was appointed to the central committee of Castro's Cuban Communist party in 1965.

Che Guevara (right) and Castro's brother Raúl at a camp in the Sierra Cristal in June 1957. The photograph was taken shortly after Raul had been appointed commander of one of the three companies into which Castro, to improve military efficiency, had divided his forces.

AP/WIDE WORLD PHOTOS

> We have been fighting for 79 days now and are stronger than ever. The [pro-Batista] soldiers are fighting badly; their morale is low, ours could not be higher.
>
> —FIDEL CASTRO

to overthrow Batista meant constant hardship. Castro and his men lived in spartan style, with little food or sleep, and only the companionship of their fellow guerrillas. Castro shared the hardships of mountain life with everyone else, but he pushed himself even harder than his companions. His ability to march for hours without rest earned him the nickname *el Caballo* ("the horse"). He traveled throughout the mountains, making contacts with peasants and winning over new allies. In Lee Lockwood's *Castro's Cuba, Cuba's Fidel*, Guillermo García, one of the first peasants to join the rebellion, is quoted: "In six months, Fidel knew the whole Sierra better than any peasant who was born here. He never forgot a place that he went to. He remembered everything — the soil, the trees, who lived in each house."

From February to late May 1957, the rebels learned what Che Guevara called the "secret" of guerrilla warfare: "constant mobility, constant distrust, constant vigilance."

Reinforcements from the cities began to reach the

rebels by late May. Among them were two women, Celia Sánchez and Vilma Espín. Castro decided the time had come to put his forces into battle. The rebels had done little militarily since landing in Oriente, and Castro worried that they would either be forgotten or given up for lost by the Cuban people.

On May 28, 1957, after a 15-day march, 80 Fidelistas attacked El Uvero, an army post guarded by 53 soldiers. The rebels fired round after round into the barracks, but the soldiers held out for nearly three hours. Losses on both sides were heavy: more than a quarter of the combatants were wounded or killed in the fierce fighting.

Guevara noted in his memoirs that the battle gave a tremendous boost to the rebels' morale. "It marked," he wrote, "our coming of age as guerrillas." El Uvero was also strategically important. Forced to dismantle its small outposts in the Sierra Maestra, the army gave up most of the mountain region of Oriente province to the rebel forces.

New York Times correspondent Herbert Matthews (1900–77) interviews Castro in the Sierra Maestra on February 17, 1958. Matthews later wrote: "The personality of the man is overpowering. . . . Here was an educated, dedicated fanatic, a man of ideals, of courage, and of remarkable qualities of leadership."

AP/WIDE WORLD PHOTOS

4

On to Havana

People of Cuba! The tyrant has fled, as have the other assassins, before the irresistible advance of the rebel army.
—announcement made on the rebel radio station, January 1, 1959

By early 1958, Castro had been in the Sierra Maestra for close to 13 months. He now commanded a 300-man guerrilla army, which could roam the Sierra at will. By March, under the leadership of Fidel's brother Raúl, the rebels had also extended their control to the Sierra Cristal, a mountainous area west of the Sierra Maestra.

The rebels, whose full beards earned them the nickname *los barbudos*, were easily recognizable. Their tattered, olive green uniforms, stiff from sweat and mud, were crisscrossed with cartridge belts and the straps of their ever-present rifles. Some wore cowboy-style hats or berets, but most of the *barbudos* favored baseball caps.

The rebels established an elaborate support network in the mountains. They commissioned the local peasants to raise beans, corn, and rice for them. They built workshops to make uniforms, knapsacks, shoes, and even cigars. They constructed an armory to repair weapons and manufacture bombs, mines, and Molotov cocktails. They laid telephone lines between 55 mountain checkpoints, which enabled them to send and receive reports about army

UPI/INTERNATIONAL NEWSPHOTOS

Rosa Herrero, a Cuban resident of New York, displays a sign announcing that she is in the 87th hour of a hunger strike on April 2, 1958. Herrero was one of many Cuban emigrés in the United States who took part in such demonstrations to express their sympathy with Castro's forces.

His trademark cigar firmly clamped between his teeth, Castro gives a new recruit some pointers on firearms in early 1958. By now, the revolutionaries were virtually self-sufficient; they manufactured most of their own supplies, from bombs to uniforms to cigars.

EASTFOTO

45

patrols entering their territory. They also published a regular newspaper. In February 1958 their own broadcasting system, *Radio Rebelde*, began transmitting. Castro made frequent broadcasts from what he called the "Territory of Free Cuba in the Sierra Maestra."

The guerrillas had a dramatic impact on the lives of the mountain peasants, or *campesinos*. They pressured sugar mill owners to increase wages; those who refused would be given 24 hours in which they could either reconsider or watch their mills burn to the ground. The rebels began to educate the illiterate *campesinos*, and their hospital treated not only their own wounded, but peasant families as well. As a result of these efforts, the rebels received widespread support in the Sierra Maestra; even members of a local leper colony became staunch Fi-

Rebel soldiers manufacture Molotov cocktails (firebombs) in March 1958, soon after the United States announced that it was suspending arms shipments to Cuba. Although the arms embargo dealt the Batista regime a punishing blow, it did not signal the end of American political support for Batista.

Creating an accessible route for vehicles, Oriente province farmers clear brush from a cowpath on March 26, 1958. The following day, Castro's forces made their first motorized assault on a government installation — a police post in Manzanillo. The rebels avoided detection by approaching their target on cowpaths and dirt roads.

delistas, contributing boxes of medical supplies to the rebel cause.

As Castro and his mountain army grew stronger, discontent continued to swell in Cuba. Revolutionary students, hoping to spark a nationwide uprising by assassinating Batista, had assaulted the presidential palace in Havana the previous spring. The student attack had been furiously crushed by government troops. In September 1957 the naval garrison at Cienfuegos mutinied and took control of the city, but the isolated rebellion was quickly defeated by troops loyal to Batista. In the cities, rebel groups continued their campaign of sabotage and bombing of government buildings.

Signs of strife were everywhere. Havana's presidential palace now resembled a besieged fortress; guards with submachine guns waved away tourists who dared approach. The city bristled with armed members of Batista's police force. The government monotonously — and inaccurately — reported tremendous army victories over rebel forces. Castro's troops were dismissed as "insignificant bandits." To get uncensored accounts of the latest battles, many Cubans simply turned their radios to *Radio Rebelde.*

A Havana switchboard operator works by the light of candles and lanterns during a blackout on April 9, 1958. The city's lights had gone out when electricity workers, responding to Castro's call for a general strike, had walked off their jobs. The rebels had hoped for a massive strike, but most union workers refused to participate.

[Fidel] wanted to go back and regroup his men. Faustino and I persuaded him to stay where he was because God knew where our comrades had scattered to. And after all, if there was one person about whom to be anxious it was he, who would lead the revolution and who would overthrow Batista. He should not risk falling into the hands of the soldiers.

—UNIVERSO SÁNCHEZ
Cuban revolutionary

In spite of press censorship, Havana's cartoonists found ways to satirize the Batista regime. One famous illustration showed a long line of people waiting to board Havana's number 30 bus. Readers realized the bus ran to a neighborhood called La Sierra, like Castro's hideout, but the censor missed the connection.

On March 14, 1958, the United States announced it was suspending arms shipments to Cuba. Washington said it took the action because Batista, violating his word, had used American weapons for internal security rather than for defense of the hemisphere. This evidence of American disapproval sent shockwaves through influential Cuban circles. The following day, Havana's business associations issued a statement calling for Batista's resignation. Batista was now almost totally isolated.

Despite its arms embargo, the United States continued to support the Batista regime; the administration of President Dwight D. Eisenhower distrusted potential revolutionary governments. In light of the Cuban rebels' outspoken plans to create a new, independent Cuban society, the United States, said U.S. ambassador to Cuba Earl Smith, would never "be able to do business with Fidel Castro."

On May 24, 1958, Batista launched a new military offensive. He sent 10,000 soldiers, supported by Sherman tanks and armored cars, to Oriente province to crush the rebel upstarts once and for all. Even against such overwhelming odds, however, the rebels had some clear advantages. Batista's troops were poorly trained, especially for mountain fighting. The rebels, on the other hand, were seasoned veterans of guerrilla warfare, and their intelligence network was far better than that of Batista's army. The rebels knew of every enemy move almost as soon as it happened.

As Batista's troops moved slowly through the mountains, rebel detachments harassed them at every turn. The further they penetrated into rebel territory, the more ambushes they suffered, and the more isolated they became from their supply lines. Batista's army was losing men rapidly, and food and ammunition were running low. Making things harder for the government troops, Castro bombarded them through loudspeakers with calls to join the rebel cause against the hated dictatorship.

One of the most important battles during the 76-day offensive occurred at El Jigüe. Intense fighting began on July 11; after several days the Batista forces, commanded by Major José Quevedo, found themselves surrounded. Cut off from reinforcements and without food and water, Quevedo's men began to lose heart. When Castro learned that Quevedo had been a fellow classmate at the university, he proposed a cease-fire, which was quickly accepted. After a talk with Castro, Quevedo told his men that surrender would be in the best interests of Cuba. His 146 soldiers accordingly laid down their arms, and the guerrillas gained a large cache of weapons.

The torrential rains of the hurricane season soon forced the government to end its offensive. On August 7 a demoralized and confused army, under constant attack by Castro's men, retreated to its garrisons, never to return to the Sierra Maestra.

With the Batista army in disarray, Castro made plans for an immediate counteroffensive, which he hoped would lead to a victorious drive to Havana. His strategy was to isolate and surround the major urban areas, and secure the remainder of Oriente province. Forces under Fidel and Raúl Castro's command would stay in Oriente and move to capture Santiago; two columns under Che Guevara and Camilo Cienfuegos would separately move westward toward Las Villas province.

> *The organization and propaganda apparatus must be so powerful that it implacably destroys anyone who tries to create splits, camarillas [cliques], schisms, or to rise against the movement.*
> —FIDEL CASTRO

AP/WIDE WORLD PHOTOS

Castro questions a man accused of stealing from Sierra Maestra farmers. The rebel leader's concern for the local peasants contrasted sharply with the Batista regime's indifference to this segment of the population.

49

It took Guevara's column 40 days to reach Las Villas. Traveling only at night, often marching through miles of knee-deep mud, the men were often hungry and always exhausted. Guevara's forces, however, were to deliver the decisive military thrust of the war. By the middle of October 1958, the column had reached Las Villas, where it joined forces with local revolutionary groups. Together, the rebel groups launched an offensive, which included a major effort to cut the roads that linked the province with the rest of the island.

In Oriente province, Castro was ready to launch his own attack on the plains, fighting for the first time outside the now familiar Sierra Maestra. Castro spent weeks going over every detail, ranging from how many fighters to commit to the attack down to who should carry the machine gun or mortar into battle. By November 1958 the threat of rebel ambushes had almost completely stopped traffic along the central highway; the road was littered with skeletons of army trucks and jeeps. Telephone and telegraph wires were down, and many cities in the province were without electricity. The guerrillas

Cuban army recruits swear allegiance to the Batista government in April 1958. The army's performance in battle against Castro's forces was disastrous. Badly trained and ineptly led, the government troops disintegrated before the rebels' superior mobility and tactics.

U.S. ambassador to Cuba Earl Smith (b. 1903) confers with Batista on July 24, 1957. Smith, a wealthy businessman, took a dim view of Castro's plans to reform Cuban society. He was convinced that the U.S. government would never "be able to do business with Castro."

seemed a more imposing force than their small numbers warranted.

On November 20, 1958, a squad of 180 rebels under Castro's direction moved against the strategic garrison at Guisa de Miranda. The rebels cut the power lines into the army barracks, and as night fell they opened up a deafening thunder of gunfire. After 15 minutes, the firing abruptly stopped. Inside the barracks, soldiers waited nervously, wondering when the next attack would come. Half an hour later, Castro's men again opened fire. Over loudspeakers, the rebels began taunting the soldiers with insults, curses, and rebel songs. They followed up with another volley of gunfire and this time mortar shells as well. Soldiers scrambled to their positions, but no attack materialized. Then the rebels began over again with their chants and songs.

This psychological warfare continued for several days. When Castro learned that troops were being sent to reinforce the garrison, he prepared an elaborate set of ambushes, complete with mines and traps. Three times, army relief columns were forced to turn back under the guerrillas' incessant fire. By December 6 the army, which had suffered over 250 casualties, decided to abandon the garrison.

Castro's troops entered Guisa to cheers from the townspeople.

Throughout the war zones, in both Oriente and Las Villas provinces, a pattern developed along the lines of the Guisa engagement. Large army garrisons in the cities were unable to break through and reinforce their compatriots besieged in the small towns. Occasionally the soldiers gave up after only a few shots because they knew the rebels would treat them fairly. As the offensives progressed, this scenario became more familiar to the demoralized men of Batista's army. They were beginning to see the handwriting on the wall.

By December 1958 the United States realized that Batista's army was crumbling. William Pawley, an American businessman with extensive interests in Cuba, was sent to Havana to try to persuade Batista to resign. The Americans hoped to replace him with a friendly "caretaker" government that would prevent Castro from coming to power. Batista was offered a home in Florida, but he rejected the plan. He insisted that his troops would quickly defeat the rebel forces.

In reality, however, rebel victory was imminent. By mid-December Guevara's forces controlled all of Las Villas province, and on December 18 they attacked the city of Santa Clara, Batista's remaining stronghold. In Oriente province, Castro and his comrades began to plan the final attack on the city of Santiago.

On December 31, after Santa Clara had fallen to Guevara's troops, Batista finally realized his situation was hopeless. At 3:00 A.M. on January 1, 1959, he and a handful of his close associates boarded an airplane for the Dominican Republic and left Cuba for good. News of his departure spread quickly through Havana. Telephone lines were jammed with people trying to call their friends. *"Se fue"* ("he left") was usually all that was needed to tell the listener what had happened.

In the early dawn, thousands of people walked the streets of Havana in a state of intense excitement. Students gathered at the university and draped campus buildings with the red and black flags of

Revolution opens the way to true merit — to those who have valor and sincere ideals, to those who carry their breast uncovered, and who take up the battle standard in their hands. To a revolutionary party there must correspond a young and revolutionary leadership, of popular origin, which will save Cuba.

—FIDEL CASTRO

the 26th of July Movement. By evening, however, the city's mood turned darker. Crowds attacked offices and buildings that symbolized the Batista regime, and the houses of Batista officials were looted by angry rioters.

When Castro learned of Batista's flight, he prepared to move on Santiago. The city's military commander, however, surrendered without a battle, and Castro entered the city in peace. From Santiago, Castro broadcast an emergency appeal to the people of Havana, urging them to refrain from violence and vigilante justice. He promised that rebel forces would move into Cuba's cities to restore order and prevent a counterrevolution by the still relatively intact Batista army. "The dictatorship has collapsed," he said, "but that does not mean the revolution has triumphed. Revolution, yes! Military coup, no!"

Increasingly confident of victory, Castro and his men salute their cause in the Sierra Maestra in September 1958. By now, the Cuban army was severely impaired by the American arms embargo, but the rebels were receiving regular shipments of weapons and other military equipment from their supporters abroad.

CUBAN COUNCIL OF STATE

A Havana policeman fires on looters leaving a Havana casino on January 1, 1959. Earlier the same day, Batista, faced with the collapse of the Cuban army's morale, had fled to the Dominican Republic. He was accompanied by his family and closest colleagues.

Castro ordered Guevara and Cienfuegos to march to Havana, and on January 2 they occupied the major army garrisons. All over Cuba, revolutionary troops took possession of government buildings, police and radio stations, and military installations. At the same time, ex-Batista officials and policemen were captured and jailed to await trial, and people imprisoned by Batista as political criminals were released. The transition was surprisingly calm. Even Castro's severe critic, American Ambassador Earl Smith, was impressed. "Under the circumstances," he said of the rebel troops, "they remained in remarkable control."

Castro set out for Havana on January 2, turning Cuba's central highway into a 500-mile-long parade. Carrying signs reading *Gracias Fidel* ("Thank You, Fidel"), people waited a day in advance along Castro's route to see Cuba's new hero. Castro reached Havana on January 8. Gathered to greet him at the presidential palace were more than half a million Cubans, some of them clinging to rooftops or perched in trees.

"I swear before my compatriots that if any of our *compañeros*, or if our movement, or if I should become an obstacle to peace, from this very moment, the people can decide about us and tell us what to do," Castro declared.

As Castro spoke, two white doves, symbols of peace, were released by the crowd. One flew to Castro's shoulder, where it remained as he continued his speech: "We cannot ever become dictators. Those who do not have the people with them must resort to being dictators. We have the love of the people, and because of that love, we will never turn away from our principles," he said.

It was clear that Castro had won his battle with Batista. What remained to be seen was how that victory would affect Cuba.

A triumphant Castro arrives in Havana on January 8, 1959. The rebel leader later addressed a large crowd of 500,000 cheering Cubans. "He seemed to weave a hypnotic net over his listeners," reported a *New York Times* correspondent, "making them believe in his own concept of the functions of government and the destiny of Cuba."

5

The Revolution Takes Command

> *We have the most wonderful plans for Cuba!*
> —FIDEL CASTRO

In 1959 power in Cuba was suddenly placed in the hands of a group of young revolutionaries (at 32, Fidel Castro was one of the oldest) completely inexperienced in every aspect of government administration. Clearly, the tasks confronting Castro after the revolution would be much more complicated than anything he had faced in the Sierra Maestra.

Compared to the fierce independence struggles against Spain in the late 1800s, there had been relatively little loss of life or destruction of property during the guerrilla conflict of the 1950s. Unlike other 20th-century revolutionaries, Castro was not faced with the tremendous task of reviving a devastated economy; both business inventories and employment were high.

Castro's temperament and his years of struggle combined to give him a style of leadership based on boundless optimism and a willingness to improvise. When he entered Havana as a conquering hero, however, Castro had only vague ideas about solving Cuba's most pressing problems. Che Guevara later commented, "We were only a group of combatants

Following Castro's lead on January 22, 1959, thousands of Cubans in Havana demonstrate their approval of revolutionary justice. Castro had asked them to show their opinion of the recent executions of "war criminals" by military courts.

UPI/BETTMANN NEWSPHOTOS

Ousted dictator Batista and his son Jorge (b. 1943) in the Dominican Republic in February 1959. After Batista's departure from Cuba, the scale of the atrocities he had authorized became clear: investigations revealed evidence of torture, execution without trial, and the burial of victims in unmarked graves.

with high ideals and little preparation . . . we had to change the structures and we began the changes without a plan." Although Castro would later ally his nation with the Soviet Union and would become the secretary general (chief executive officer) of the Cuban Communist party, he was not a party member at the time of the revolution. He went out of his way, in fact, to emphasize this point, often noting that the Cuban rebels were "neither capitalists nor communists, but humanists," or that they opposed both "capitalist freedom without bread" and "communist bread without freedom."

Some of the rebel groups — particularly those

A revolutionary official exhibits the contents of a safe-deposit box left behind by Batista when he fled Cuba in January 1959. During his years in power, Batista had amassed an illegal fortune estimated at $300 million. Most of the money he stole was invested abroad.

UPI/BETTMANN NEWSPHOTOS

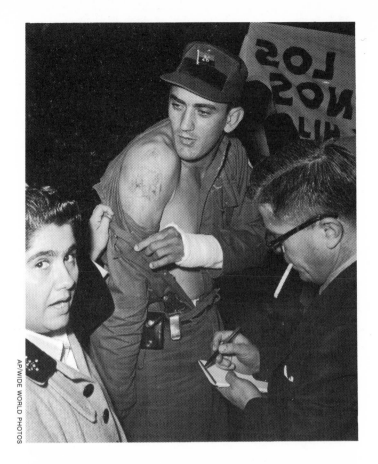

Describing the torture he suffered at the hands of Batista's police, Enrique Peraza shows scars left by a hot branding iron. The Cuban rebel soldier was testifying at a January 18, 1959, meeting staged by Cuban women to demonstrate their support for the execution of war criminals.

in the cities — that helped the 26th of July Movement topple Batista were composed of bona fide communists. Others were radical students who, ideologically sympathetic to Castro, supported the revolution. The Communist party itself had no active involvement.

The exact point at which Castro adopted communism as his political creed is difficult to pinpoint, but after he officially embraced communism, he indicated that he had been a longtime Marxist. In any case, he welcomed whatever support he could get in the late 1950s, including that of the communists.

In those first magical days of 1959, the revolution seemed to be the fulfillment of everyone's dreams; almost anything seemed possible. Portraits of Castro were now prominently displayed alongside those of saints in poor homes, and small statues of the

Castro is sworn in as prime minister by President Manuel Urrutia (left; 1901–81) on February 16, 1959.

revolutionary leader were sold on every street corner. School buildings and government institutions were renamed in honor of the heroes of the revolution. Even the business community joined in the salutes to the revolution. The National Association of Coffee Growers sent this telegram: "To the glorious rebel army: Just as yesterday we were at your side in the mountains . . . today we are with you to consolidate the Fatherland." And, of course, throughout Latin America, Castro's victory sparked the imaginations of countless would-be revolutionaries.

For the first provisional government, which was to run the country until elections were held 18 months later, Castro selected moderate, middle-class, middle-aged men with anti-Batista records. Manuel Urrutia, a former judge, was appointed president; other key cabinet posts, such as secretary of state, president of the Bank of Cuba, and minister of foreign affairs, were also given to men from this fairly conservative older generation. Only two members of the 26th of July Movement were in this first cabinet. Castro himself was a member of the government only by virtue of his position as commander in chief of the rebel army. Castro did not attend any cabinet meetings at first and, indeed, seemed reluctant to become actively involved in the affairs of the government.

Castro preferred to take part in "direct government," involving constant contact with the people. Day after day, night after night, four or five hours at a time, television and radio stations broadcast his impassioned voice and dramatic image to every city, town, and village in Cuba. Castro's bearded face appeared so often on television that he began to resemble, according to author Hugh Thomas, "a kind of permanent confessor, a revolutionary medicine man."

Castro was a natural orator. He never prepared his speeches in advance, relying only on his eloquence and ebullient personality to hold his audiences' attention and convey his message. In *Castro's Cuba, Cuba's Fidel*, author Lee Lockwood quotes Castro on his speech-making style: "If you try to give a definite shape to your ideas, to give them a prior form, when you begin to speak, you lose one of the finest influences that the public can exercise over the person who speaks, which is to transmit its order, its enthusiasm, its force, its inspiration through him. Often my speeches are conversations . . . with the public."

Revolutionary army officers preside at the January 12, 1959, trial of former Batista henchmen accused of torture and murder. Castro's military courts, which frequently handed out death sentences, were widely criticized abroad. Most of the critics — including the United States — had remained silent about the Batista regime's human rights abuses.

Found guilty of war crimes by a revolutionary tribunal, Aristidies Díaz, a supporter of the Batista regime, is comforted by a priest as he awaits his death by firing squad in Manzanillo on January 12, 1958. Lining the road are the bodies of men executed earlier.

The provisional government's earliest measures were more reformist than revolutionary. It lowered rents, and set new wage levels. It replaced the executives in government agencies with prorevolutionary officials, and saw to it that the newspaper *Revolución* published detailed accounts of corruption in high places during the Batista regime. The new government also vigorously attacked such Batista mainstays as gambling and prostitution.

The new government was popular. Its members were known for their hard work and scrupulous avoidance of graft. "For the first time," said Castro, "there are worthy men at the head of the country who neither sell themselves nor falter nor are intimidated by any threat."

In early February, the provisional prime minister

resigned and Castro assumed the post. It soon became evident that there were two governments in Cuba: one located in the offices of the president and the cabinet, the other wherever Castro happened to be at the time. Castro, who kept three separate residences, rarely settled down for any length of time, and ministers or department chiefs often had a hard time tracking him down. One of his supporters commented that given Castro's unconventional style and lack of interest in formal procedures, it seemed as if everything of importance in Cuba happened late at night or at dawn. Castro would often arrive hours late for cabinet meetings, having already made most of the important policy decisions beforehand after behind-the-scenes discussions with his closest advisers.

After Batista's departure, most of his regime's leading police and military officers fled, went into hiding, or were arrested. Police stations and pro-

Castro meets with U.S. Vice-President Richard M. Nixon (b. 1913) in Washington, D.C., on April 19, 1959. Castro publicly disavowed communism during this visit, but Nixon later wrote: "I was convinced Castro was either incredibly naïve about communism or under communist discipline and that we would have to treat him accordingly."

Making an unscheduled stop during his 1959 visit to the United States, Castro inspects a Bengal tiger at New York City's Bronx Zoo. The official U.S. reception of the Cuban leader had been chilly, but many ordinary Americans were both impressed by his achievements and delighted by his informality.

vincial army garrisons were put under the command of trusted members of the rebel army. The horror of the Batista era now became fully apparent for the first time. As torture chambers, mutilated skeletons, and unmarked cemeteries were discovered, demands for retribution rose. The nation demonstrated a collective desire for justice.

There were some hasty court-martials in the weeks that followed the revolution. Raúl Castro, for example, ordered the execution of a number of military prisoners in Santiago. Responding to charges that the revolutionary government was conducting a bloodbath, Raúl replied that each of the 100 men in question had received a trial; 25 had been acquitted, the rest sentenced to death. "There had been a stream of widows, fathers, and mothers coming to us demanding justice," he said. "Not a single person in Santiago ever protested about what I did."

After the early wave of quick military trials, those accused of war crimes were tried by courts made up of rebel army officers and local civilians; prosecutors and defense counsels were appointed by the government. By most accounts, the trials were fair; genuine efforts were made to determine guilt or innocence.

One notable exception was in March 1959, when 44 Batista air force pilots, accused of deliberately bombing civilians, were tried and acquitted in Santiago. Following public protest against the verdict, Castro forced a retrial with a specially chosen prosecutor and judges. This time the pilots were found guilty and sentenced to 20 to 30 years of imprisonment. "Revolutionary justice," Castro argued, "is based not upon legal precepts, but on moral conviction."

The war-criminal trials were vigorously condemned in the United States by the Eisenhower administration, members of Congress, and the press. The American criticism, which was deeply resented in Cuba, inspired Castro's first verbal attack on the United States. On January 22, 1959, thousands of Cubans gathered in front of the presidential palace to demonstrate their support for the government's policy on war crimes. Castro denounced the United States for criticizing the war trials when it had remained silent about the atrocities committed by the Batista regime. He said that Cubans bore no ill will toward Americans, but that they resented attacks on them by "interests who fear the revolution." Facing the huge crowd, Castro asked everybody who approved of revolutionary justice to raise their hands. The plaza was transformed into a sea of waving arms. "The jury of a million Cubans of all ideas and social classes," said Castro, "has voted."

Castro's displeasure with the United States did not keep him from accepting an invitation to address the Washington Press Club. On April 15 he was greeted at the Washington airport by a large, cheering crowd. Some U.S. observers believed Castro's visit would include traditional speeches of praise for American democracy and generosity, followed by a request for massive aid. When reporters asked Castro if he came to seek foreign aid, however, he said, "No, we are proud to be independent and have no intention of asking anyone for anything." Indeed, Castro had instructed his finance ministers to refrain from asking for any assistance. He believed that U.S. officials would be more likely to offer aid to Cuba if none were requested.

Castro gave speeches in New York, Washington, and Princeton, N.J., impressing audiences with his friendly sentiments about Americans and his ability to make jokes in English. He visited universities, liberal organizations, a New York zoo, Yankee Stadium; he ate hot dogs and hamburgers. The press enthusiastically covered his every move. With his tousled hair and shaggy beard, dressed in his by now familiar wrinkled, olive-green uniform, the disarmingly eccentric Castro stood in favorable contrast to the stiffly formal foreign leaders Americans were accustomed to. One of the few protests encountered on the trip was staged by a man who picketed Castro's Washington hotel with a sign that read, "We don't like beards! BARBERS OF AMERICA."

President Eisenhower was conspicuously absent during Castro's visit, but the Cuban leader did meet with Vice-President Richard Nixon. Nixon presented Castro with files, compiled by the Central Intelligence Agency (CIA), purporting to show that some of Castro's supporters were communists. Castro's apparent lack of interest in the files displeased the vice-president. Nixon's concern with communism was mirrored in the American press. CBS, for example, broadcast a program entitled "Is Cuba Going Red?" The show strongly implied that Cuba was becoming a communist dictatorship.

Castro, who had publicly announced that he was not a communist, was annoyed by the constant questions on the subject. It seemed to him and his entourage that the United States was not really concerned with what Cuba was so long as it was not communist. In a speech after he returned to Havana Castro said, "Anyone who doesn't sell out or knuckle under is smeared as a communist. As for me, I am not selling out to the Americans nor will I take orders from the Americans." After he had officially swung toward the communist camp, Castro claimed he had been a communist all along. Whether this is the case, or whether he was still on the fence at the time of his U.S. visit is an unanswerable question.

While Castro visited the United States, Che Guevara was making a round-the-world trip aimed at getting international support for Cuba. He was warmly received in India, Japan, Indonesia, Burma, Yugoslavia, and Morocco. Guevara proclaimed Cuban neutrality in the U.S.-Soviet Cold War, and linked Cuba with the underdeveloped nations of the Third World. Talking about Cuba's foreign policy, he said, "In the chess game of power politics, you will never find us playing the part of a docile pawn."

Chinese Communist leader Mao Zedong (right; 1893–1976) welcomes Che Guevara to Beijing on November 19, 1960. During his visit, Guevara expressed admiration for the communists' success in the Chinese civil war (1927–49). "The Chinese people in their 22 years of struggle," he said, had "revealed a new road for the Americas."

6

The Revolution Under Attack

The Cuban government's wish to remain independent in foreign affairs was matched by a desire to achieve political stability and economic security at home. Castro liked to quote a saying of José Martí: "Without economic independence, there can be no political independence."

Cuba's economy — before and after the revolution — was based on agriculture. The nation's most important crop was sugar, whose production employed more than a third of the labor force. Sugarcane fields covered more than one-quarter of the country, and sugar accounted for more than 80 percent of its exports.

At the time of the revolution, most of Cuba's sugar-producing land was owned or controlled by a small number of individuals or companies, many of them based in the United States. Some of the nation's peasant farmers owned tiny plots of land; others rented the ground they tilled or worked as sharecroppers — receiving part of the crops they produced in return for cultivating land owned by others. Life in the countryside was wretched: few

AP/WIDE WORLD PHOTOS

Castro signs the Agrarian Reform law on May 17, 1959. The new law authorized the seizure and redistribution of all farms larger than 1,000 acres. The legislation appalled Cuba's wealthier landowners, who immediately began a campaign of economic sabotage.

Castro cuts sugarcane on a plantation in southern Cuba in 1962. As part of its program of economic sanctions, the United States reduced its imports of Cuban sugar in 1960. From that point on, Cuba exported most of its sugar to the Soviet Union.

peasants could provide meat for their families' tables, only about half could read or write, and almost none had access to running water or electricity.

From the beginning of the 26th of July Movement, Castro had listed land reform as one of the principal objectives of the revolution. He had promised that the new government would give land to the landless peasants, or more land to those with very small farms. He had also promised to pay the previous owners for the land expropriated, or taken over, by the government.

On May 17, 1959, at La Plata, the site of one of the rebel army's earliest victories, Castro unveiled a new farmland reform law. Almost all farms were now limited to a maximum size of 1,000 acres. (The exceptions were those that produced at least 50 percent more crops per acre than the national average.)

The first Cuban peasant to receive redistributed property under the terms of the Agrarian Reform law accepts title to his new land from Castro in 1959.

EASTFOTO

All property over the 1,000-acre limit was to be expropriated by the government and its owners compensated by 20-year guaranteed bonds. Some of the expropriated land would be distributed to individual peasants, and some would be turned over to agricultural cooperatives. The cooperatives, or state farms, would be operated by a new agency, the Institute of Agrarian Reform (INRA). INRA quickly became one of the most important institutions in revolutionary Cuba. As well as expropriating and redistributing the land, it organized the construction of roads, health clinics, schools, and housing.

Until the land reform program was put into effect, criticism of the government had been relatively moderate. Potential opponents had been restrained by Castro's extraordinary popularity and his remarkable ability to shape public opinion. Agrarian reform, however, directly threatened the interests of powerful sectors of Cuban society, and triggered the first substantial open opposition to the Castro regime. In early June, the government seized 131 large cattle ranches near the city of Camagüey. Among them were several estates owned by United States firms and by wealthy Cuban families. Reacting to the expropriation, the cattle ranchers purchased time on radio and television to attack the government. They also resorted to economic sabotage: excessive slaughter of livestock, overharvesting of crops, poor maintenance, and underinvestment in production.

Along with these protests, Castro was confronted by the spectre of communism now raised by his opponents. The conservative newspaper *Diario de la Marina* compared the Fidelistas with watermelons — "green on the outside [the color of their uniforms] and red on the inside." On June 29 Pedro Díaz Lanz, the chief of the Cuban air force, gave a press conference in which he spoke about the dangers of communism. Severely reproached for his remarks by Castro, Díaz Lanz gathered his family together and departed for Florida. On July 13 President Urrutia publicly attacked the Cuban Communist party, which, he said, was "inflicting terrible harm on Cuba." Urrutia's speech was aimed

> The [Cuban] movement is not a communist movement. Its members are Roman Catholic mostly. . . . We have no intention of expropriating U.S. property, and any property we take we'll pay for.
> —FIDEL CASTRO
> speaking in 1959

Leading Cuban revolutionary Hubert Matos (left; b. 1923) strides past Cuban guards following his October 24, 1959, arrest on Castro's orders. Furious over Castro's appointment of Cuban Communist party members to the revolutionary government, Matos had resigned as governor of Camagüey province a few days earlier.

at forcing Castro to denounce the Cuban communists publicly.

On July 17, when Cubans opened their morning newspaper, *Revolución*, they found an amazing headline: Fidel Castro had resigned his position as prime minister. The announcement took even Castro's closest associates by surprise. Castro, who had told no one of his plans, had gone to the newspaper's printing office himself to compose his resignation. That night, he went on television and delivered a blistering attack on Urrutia. The president, he said, was spreading rumors of communism in order to provoke aggression from abroad. Castro believed that strongly anticommunist views indicated sympathy with the United States — and, therefore, opposition to the revolution. Incensed by Urrutia's outspoken views, Castro deliberately stirred the public into demanding his resignation.

As Castro spoke on television, huge crowds gathered in the streets to call for Urrutia's departure. The next day, Urrutia resigned his position. After this, Castro would make no more anticommunist statements in his speeches or private conversations. He would, on the contrary, reserve his criticism for those who were anticommunists. "All revolutionary sectors must support the Revolution," he said. "We need to keep control in our hands or the Revolution will fall apart as in 1933. And nobody presented us with power as a gift."

As well as believing that anticommunism was simply a pretext for opposing the revolution, Castro felt that he needed the support of Cuba's well-organized Communist party. He had rushed headlong into agrarian reform without experienced, trained personnel to administer the new system. He could count on the loyalty of his close associates, but this was only a small, youthful group, and its members were not skilled administrators. The Cuban Communist party, on the other hand, had over 15,000 members, many of them older people with years of political and administrative experience. The Communist party, as Castro said later, "had men who were truly revolutionary, loyal, honest, and trained. I needed them."

Soon after Urrutia's resignation, a new president was sworn in. He was Osvaldo Dorticós, a well-to-do lawyer who had quietly supported the revolution. Castro then announced that he would let the public decide his own political future. A public meeting was scheduled in Havana on July 26. The rally was attended by most of the city's residents as well as by thousands of peasants who had walked in from the countryside. Dorticós proclaimed that the people demanded Castro's return to the prime ministership. His assertion was not exaggerated: wild cheering, dancing in the streets, and shouts of "*Viva Fidel!*" followed his words. Accepting his renewed mandate, Castro gave a four-hour speech — a fairly short address for the eloquent revolutionary.

Castro's popularity was unquestionable, but rumblings of dissatisfaction continued. Small counter-revolutionary guerrilla groups began to spring up in the Sierra de Escambray, and in mid-August a plot against the government by cattle ranchers in Las Villas was uncovered. Fifty members of the "invading force" organized by the disgruntled cattlemen were arrested, along with some 2,000 of their suspected supporters.

In mid-October 1959 Hubert Matos, the military governor of Camagüey and Castro's old comrade-in-arms, resigned from his office. He made it clear that his move was prompted by his dismay over the increasing influence of communists on the government. Following Matos's lead, most of the province's military officers also left the government. A vital area of the country appeared to be defecting, and the threat of a military uprising seemed possible. Convinced that the revolution was endangered, and enraged by his former ally's defection, Castro denounced Matos as "a traitor who had obstructed agrarian reform." Castro personally arrested Matos, who was later tried for "antirevolutionary conduct," found guilty, and sentenced to 20 years in prison.

Soon after Matos's arrest, the ex-commander of the Cuban air force, Díaz Lanz, piloted a B-25 bomber from Florida to Havana and dropped thousands of leaflets asserting that Castro was a communist. Trying to shoot Díaz Lanz's plane down, a Cuban aircraft accidentally dropped several bombs, which killed two people and wounded 45 on the ground. The Havana newspaper *Revolución* headlined its report of the incident "THE AIRPLANES CAME FROM THE U.S." Castro, who charged that the civilians had been killed and injured by bombs dropped by Díaz Lanz, addressed a crowd of 500,000 in Havana two days later. "What reason have they for attacking Cuba?" he asked. "What crime have we committed? What have the Cuban people done to merit such attacks?"

As members of his government continued their violent debate about the degree of authority that should be allowed to Cuba's communists, Castro chose to intensify the revolutionary process. Medium-sized agricultural estates were now targeted for expropriation, more cattle ranches were seized, and new laws provided firmer controls and higher taxes for foreign-owned businesses. The cabinet was reorganized, with most of the liberal (noncommunist) ministers replaced by loyal *Fidelistas*.

As 1959 drew to a close, tension in Cuba was mounting. Matos's treason trial was the first of many. A number of Cuban and North American

Former Cuban air force commander Pedro Luis Díaz Lanz (b. 1936). Protesting what he called communist infiltration of Cuba's armed forces, Díaz Lanz had resigned his post on June 30, 1959, and fled to the United States. Four months later, he flew a B-25 bomber over Havana and dropped thousands of leaflets accusing Castro of being a communist.

AP/WIDE WORLD PHOTOS

The wreckage of the *Le Coubre*, a French freighter that exploded in Havana harbor on March 4, 1960. Although the cause of the disaster — which killed 75 Cuban dockworkers and injured 200 others — was unknown, Castro immediately accused the U.S. government of sabotaging the ship.

"counterrevolutionaries" were given stiff sentences after trials that some observers regarded as unfair. The government crackdown on those who disagreed with its policies created an atmosphere of suspicion. This was heightened by reports of increasing anti-Castro guerrilla activities in the mountains and sabotage in the cities. By year's end, Castro was predicting an invasion of Cuba, and he began plans to organize a students' and workers' militia to meet the threat. He told a convention of sugar workers: "We shall have to defend the revolution with arms in 1960 . . . we must become psychologically prepared to fight against great odds . . . we shall fight to the last man."

Adding to the revolutionary government's unease was its deteriorating relationship with the United States. The 1902 Platt Amendment to the Cuban constitution, which permitted unlimited U.S. intervention in Cuba's affairs, had been annulled in 1934. Cuba had nevertheless remained heavily dependent on the United States economically. The island's main source of revenue was sugar, virtually its only exportable product. The United States had traditionally purchased almost all of Cuba's sugar, buying a regular quota, or fixed amount, at guaranteed high prices.

75

Addressing a huge crowd outside Havana's presidential palace on October 26, 1959, Castro condemns American policy toward Cuban exiles. He accused the United States of permitting the exiles to use Florida airfields as bases for their bombing runs over Cuban sugar plantations and government installations.

Ever since the Cuban revolution, the United States had been growing increasingly apprehensive about the political situation in its small southern neighbor. The expropriation of American property and the high tariffs (taxes) Castro had placed on goods imported from the United States disturbed Americans. Most alarming, however, were reports of mushrooming communist influence in Cuba.

On its part, Cuba was extremely worried about the potential hostility of the United States, particularly in terms of sugar exports. In mid-December 1959 the American secretary of state, Christian Herter, remarked ominously that he was considering what the United States "might do to the sugar quota if Cuba doesn't calm down."

In spite of his concern about the U.S. sugar market, Castro began to make speeches attacking the United States and accusing it of trying to destroy the Cuban revolution. Instead of continuing to insist that Cuba was neither communist nor capitalist, he now made no effort to deny the strength of the communist movement in Cuba. He told associates he believed that North American fears of communism in Cuba gave Cuba additional leverage in its dealings with the United States.

Although Eisenhower was being pressured to assist the U.S.-based Cuban exiles who hoped to overthrow Castro, he decided to make an effort to reestablish cordial relations with Cuba. Through ambassadors, he suggested that Cuba stop its campaign of verbal warfare against the United States and work with the American ambassador toward resolving differences between the two countries. The United States, in return, would offer financial assistance to Cuba.

At the same time, however, Cuban exiles were using Florida as a base from which to make small-scale bombing runs over Cuba. The raids, at this time, were not supported by the United States, but neither were they stopped, and they fanned the flames of resentment in Cuba.

In February 1960 the Soviet deputy premier, Anastas Mikoyan, visited Cuba to open a new era of Cuban-Soviet relations. The Soviet Union agreed to buy substantial amounts of Cuban sugar over the next five years, and to provide Cuba with needed supplies and technical aid.

Relations between the United States (displeased with the Cuban-Soviet agreements) and Cuba (distressed by the exiles' raids) were thus already tense when an unexpected incident strained them to the breaking point. On March 4 a French freighter, the *Le Coubre*, which had been delivering rifles and grenades from Belgium to Cuba, blew up in Havana harbor. Seventy-five Cuban dockworkers were killed and 200 injured. The cause of the explosion was never discovered, but Castro promptly blamed it on the United States. "You," he said to the North American nation, "will reduce us neither by war nor by famine." The United States just as quickly denied responsibility for the disaster, but the possibility of friendly U.S.-Cuban relations had exploded along with the *Le Coubre*.

A few weeks after the explosion, Eisenhower approved a plan, proposed by the CIA, to recruit and train anti-Castro Cuban exiles for an invasion of Cuba. Castro, the CIA had asserted, was consolidating a "communist dictatorship in Cuba." By late March, bombings of Cuban sugarcane fields and government installations were occurring on an almost daily basis. All the flights originated in the United States. "Put yourself in our place," said Castro to the Americans. "Suppose planes based in Cuba went over and dropped leaflets or even bombs on Washington. Suppose we harbored men in our country and had elements in our government who encouraged criminals and revolutionaries plotting to overthrow the United States government. How would you feel? How do you think Cubans feel?"

The downhill slide of U.S.-Cuban relations now began to speed up. In late May 1960 the Cuban government requested the three largest U.S.-owned oil refineries in Cuba to process a shipment of crude oil from the Soviet Union. The American companies, under pressure from the U.S. government, refused. In late June the U.S. House of Representatives passed a bill sharply reducing the imports of Cuban sugar. Castro, calling the move a "declaration of

Clifford Drake (left), general manager of the Texaco oil company in Cuba, receives a copy of Castro's decree ordering confiscation of all Texaco property in Cuba on June 30, 1960. Castro ordered the seizure of Cuba's U.S.-owned oil companies after they refused to process a shipment of crude oil from the Soviet Union.

economic war," responded with an ultimatum: if the American refineries continued in their refusal to process the Soviet oil, Cuba would seize them. When the oil arrived, the American refinery managers fled, and the companies were expropriated by the Cuban government.

A week later, Eisenhower signed the bill reducing the sugar quota. "This action," he said, "amounts to economic sanctions against Cuba. Now we must look ahead to other moves — economic, diplomatic, strategic."

Soviet leader Nikita Khrushchev quickly reacted to this development. In July he announced that the Soviet Union would buy the sugar rejected by the United States. He also indicated that the Soviet Union was ready to give Cuba military assistance if necessary. In the following weeks, most U.S. companies in Cuba — along with many enterprises privately owned by Cubans — were nationalized.

In mid-September 1960 Castro, leading a large group of Cuban officials, flew to New York to attend the 15th-anniversary celebration of the United Nations. Ever the master showman, the revolutionary leader became the center of attention during the ceremonies. Rejecting the fashionable hotel assigned to his delegation, Castro moved his group to a hotel in Harlem, the center of New York's black community. A number of Third World leaders attending the United Nations meeting — including Gamal Abdel Nasser of Egypt and Jawaharlal Nehru of India — went with Khrushchev to Harlem to meet with Castro. Khrushchev greeted Castro with an

Relaxing with friends in September 1960, Castro enjoys an after-dinner cigar at the Hotel Theresa in New York City's Harlem. The Cuban leader found his second visit to the United States less agreeable than his first: reports of his government's increasingly left-wing orientation had begun to turn American public opinion against him.

UPI/BETTMANN NEWSPHOTOS

Castro and Soviet Premier Nikita Khrushchev (1894–1971) embrace at the United Nations on September 20, 1960. Although this was the two leaders' first in-person meeting, they were already allies: two months earlier, Khrushchev had agreed to buy most of Cuba's sugar and to supply the island nation with military assistance.

enthusiastic Russian bear hug; the photograph of the two leaders' laughing embrace would later appear on walls all over Cuba as a symbol of Soviet-Cuban friendship. When a reporter asked Khrushchev about U.S. policy toward Cuba, the Soviet leader said, "Fidel Castro is not a communist now, but United States policies will make him one within two years."

One year later, Castro indeed proclaimed himself a communist. By late 1960 Cuba, for all practical purposes, had become a socialist state.

7

Crisis Management

The Cuban Revolution cast a large shadow over American politics. Cuba became a central topic during the 1960 presidential election. Democratic candidate John F. Kennedy, whom Castro had called an "illiterate and ignorant millionaire," accused the Eisenhower administration of allowing a "communist menace" to enter the Western hemisphere. "We must make clear our intention to enforce the Monroe Doctrine," Kennedy said. "We will not be content until democracy is restored to Cuba. The forces fighting for freedom in exile and in the mountains of Cuba should be sustained and assisted." Vice-President Nixon, Kennedy's Republican opponent, wanted to keep plans for Cuba's invasion secret. As the campaign began to wind down, however, both candidates were loudly pledging support for anti-Castro forces.

Eisenhower halted all U.S. exports to Cuba in October. Castro in turn seized the remaining U.S.-owned companies in Cuba. Convinced that the United States would invade Cuba before Eisenhower left office on January 21, Castro ordered all but a few members of the American embassy staff

Anti-Castro Cuban exiles train at a Caribbean camp shortly before their April 17, 1961, invasion of Cuba. Cuba's armed forces responded to the crisis with speed and efficiency; completely surrounded by April 19, the invaders had no choice but to surrender.

Striking a characteristic pose, Castro addresses a massive Havana audience. The Cuban leader's remarkable speaking ability — always one of his most valuable political assets — often enabled him to secure public approval for potentially unpopular government policies.

EASTFOTO

to leave Cuba. On January 3, 1961, the United States broke off diplomatic relations with Cuba.

Castro warned the United States that an invasion would be a fight to the death. He intensified militia training. "We will even arm the cats," Castro joked, "if we only can teach them how to handle a gun."

Kennedy had been informed about the secret invasion plans shortly after his election in November. In the first few days of his administration, he was still largely undecided about whether to go ahead with the invasion. The new president feared that, successful or not, a military intervention in Cuba would result in a moral and political setback for the United States in Latin America and other Third World nations.

The new administration, including the secretaries of state and defense, Dean Rusk and Robert McNamara, supported the invasion however, and CIA chief Allen Dulles assured Kennedy it would be greeted by a popular uprising against Castro. To a large extent, Kennedy was trapped by his own hardline rhetoric during the presidential campaign. Canceling an invasion that he had so wholeheartedly endorsed would open his administration to severe criticism from Congress and the press. With all these factors in mind, Kennedy ordered the CIA to continue its preparations for the invasion.

By mid-March practically everything about the invasion except its time and location was public knowledge. The CIA had stepped up its arms drops to the counterrevolutionaries in Cuba's mountains, and sabotage in the nation's cities had increased. On March 13 Kennedy unveiled his plan for the Alliance for Progress, a new multimillion-dollar aid package for Latin American countries. It was clear to most observers the announcement was timed to build up goodwill in Latin America before Cuba was invaded.

On April 15, 1961, several airplanes, piloted by Cuban exiles, bombed Cuban airfields and military quarters. Because Castro had hidden his small fleet of military aircraft and placed decoy planes in full view, damage to the air force was slight, although seven people were killed and 44 wounded in the

What bothers the United States the most is that we have made a socialist revolution right under their noses. Workers and peasants, comrades, this is a socialist and democratic revolution of the poor, by the poor, and for the poor.
—FIDEL CASTRO

attack. Throughout Cuba, the police began to round up everyone even suspected of having antigovernment sentiments.

An invasion force of 1,500 men embarked for Cuba from Puerto Cabezas, Nicaragua, on the night of April 16. Anastasio Somoza, the dictator of Nicaragua, jokingly asked the men to bring him some hairs plucked from Castro's beard. Their group's destination was the Bay of Pigs, located on the southern coast of Cuba, alongside vast stretches of treacherous swampland. The CIA assumed that once a beachhead was established, the invaders would be hard to dislodge. Between the beach and the swamp, a small strip of land contained an airfield and adequate space for a command post. Artillery and tanks would be used to seal off the area. The invasion's planners, confident that the Cuban air force had been destroyed, believed that the landing site would be immune from air attack. It would prove to be a devastatingly wrong assumption.

The invaders met with heavy resistance as soon as the first landing craft reached shore on the morning of April 17. The local militia had been alerted by sentries and went immediately into action. They also informed an army battalion stationed 20 miles

I am a Marxist-Leninist and will be one until the day I die.
—FIDEL CASTRO
speaking in 1961

Bomb-damaged trucks at Cuba's Camp Libertad barracks, near Havana, April 15, 1961. Two days before the U.S.-backed invasion of Cuba, aircraft piloted by Cuban exiles had bombed airfields and other military installations throughout the island.

UPI/BETTMANN NEWSPHOTOS

inland about the attack. Although their landing site did have several strategic advantages, the invaders overlooked a crucial factor: the revolution had markedly improved the lives of much of the Cuban population, which was, therefore, intensely loyal to the Castro regime.

Castro learned of the invasion at 3:15 A.M. and immediately flew to the area to direct military operations. Militias from nearby provinces and additional army battalions were mobilized. Castro's first crucial task was to decide how to commit the Cuban air force to the battle. His infantry lacked antiaircraft equipment and had already taken severe punishment from enemy bombing and strafing. Castro, however, decided to leave his infantry unprotected and to attack the enemy ships offshore, which were still in the process of sending supplies to the invaders. The Cuban air force delivered a crushing blow to the invading force, sinking several ships and forcing the survivors to retreat far off the coast.

By the following day, April 18, the invaders were surrounded. Realizing that the invasion had failed completely, President Kennedy refused to commit American marines to the battle or to allow U.S. planes to make air strikes against Cuban forces. By dawn on the 19th, the defenders began closing in on the beleaguered invaders. Castro's forces eventually captured 1,180 prisoners: 129 invaders had been killed. Although Castro announced that only 87 of his men died in the fighting, other estimates place Cuba's losses as high as 1,200 dead and 2,000 wounded. In any case, Castro announced, "The invaders have been annihilated. The revolution has emerged victorious."

A few days after their capture, the prisoners were brought to a sports arena where Castro conducted a five-hour televised discussion with them. The subjects included a wide range of social and political issues. One prisoner charged that Castro had "salted away a lot of money in Swiss banks"; another argued that democracy would be better for Cuba than socialism; a third said Castro had betrayed the dreams of the revolution. Castro spoke about the dramatic improvement in Cuban society since the

> *I would have taken a harder line than Khrushchev. I was furious when he compromised. But Khrushchev was older and wiser. I realize in retrospect that he reached the proper settlement with Kennedy. If my position had prevailed there might have been a terrible war.*
> —FIDEL CASTRO
> on the Cuban Missile Crisis

Cuban militiamen prepare to engage the enemy during the 1961 invasion of Cuba. In an impassioned speech before the invasion began, Castro said: "Let us form battalions . . . with the conviction that to die for our country is to live and that to live in chains is to live under the yoke of infamy and insult."

revolution and remarked that the debate itself represented a large departure from everyday politics. "Now be honest," he said, "surely you must realize that you are the first prisoners in history who have the privilege of arguing . . . with the head of a government which you came to overthrow."

In *Castro's Revolution*, Theodore Draper writes that "The ill-fated invasion of Cuba in April 1961 was one of those rare politico-military events — a perfect failure." The United States not only miscalculated the strength of Castro's popular support, but also the military capability and leadership of the revolutionary government.

The Bay of Pigs fiasco was a personal triumph for Fidel Castro and a political watershed for the Cuban revolution. The counterrevolution had received a heavy blow, and both Cuba's national pride and Castro's popularity were greater than ever. Perhaps even more important, the Cuban revolution was for the first time publicly proclaimed as a socialist revolution. On May 1, 1961, Castro announced that Cuba was a "Marxist-Leninist state." He added that there would be no more formal elections; since the revolutionary government expressed the will of the people, every day, he said, was an election day.

In one respect, the invasion could not have come at a more opportune moment. In 1961 Cuba was faced with grave economic difficulties. After the nationalizations had begun in 1960, most of the nation's top administrative, managerial, and technical personnel (primarily Americans or Cubans trained by the Americans) had left the country. Responsibility for a complex economy was now in the hands of young, dedicated, but inexperienced leaders. It was a situation that led, as Castro himself put it, to "anybody at all becoming a manager. There were times when even the village idiot was managing a sugar mill."

Because of this lack of economic managers, only half of the fruit and vegetable crops were gathered before they spoiled, rice production and sugarcane planting suffered, and an unnecessary slaughter of livestock occurred. The resulting food shortages gave rise to a rationing system in 1962. Although there was some grumbling about economic problems, the surge in Castro's popularity following the

Would-be shoppers line up at a Havana grocery store in April 1964. Rationing was instituted in Cuba in 1962, when declining agricultural production severely limited the nation's food supply. The crisis was caused by a shortage of managerial and technical personnel, many of whom had fled Cuba when the nationalization program began in 1960.

Cuban troops inspect an enemy aircraft shot down during the invasion mounted by Cuban exiles in 1961. Castro's deployment of the Cuban air force against the invaders' transport vessels was crucial to the defenders' success; the move left the exiles completely stranded.

Bay of Pigs invasion kept public dissatisfaction to a minimum.

Tension between Cuba and the United States intensified in 1962. In January the Organization of American States, responding to an American request, expelled Cuba as a member, citing its "revolutionary belligerency" in the region. In the United States, the Republicans served notice that they would make Kennedy's failure to eliminate Castro a major issue in the November congressional elections. Within Cuba, hints of a new invasion abounded: antirevolutionary groups were again engaging in acts of sabotage and guerrilla raids. In April the U.S. Navy and Marines held unusually large military maneuvers in the Caribbean.

On July 26, in a ceremony celebrating the ninth anniversary of the attack on Moncada, Castro spoke fervently about an impending U.S. invasion as though it were a foregone conclusion. In reality, no actual prospect of a second invasion existed, but the continued U.S. political and economic offensive against the revolution kept Cuba in a state of anxiety.

It was a time when we felt ourselves in danger from the United States. We consulted the Russians — which is to say, Nikita Khrushchev — on what should be done. When they suggested the missiles, we immediately said, "Yes, by all means, we are completely in accord; this satisfies our desires 100 percent."
—FIDEL CASTRO

U.S President John F. Kennedy (1917–63) meets the press after ordering a naval blockade of Cuba on October 22, 1962. The president acted after U.S. intelligence agents reported the presence of Soviet nuclear missiles in Cuba.

The hostility between Cuba and the United States emphasized the importance of Cuba's new relationship with the Soviet Union. While Castro had once hoped to stay independent in the Cold War between the United States and the Soviet Union, he now aligned himself firmly with the Soviet camp. In a late 1961 television broadcast he stated that he was a confirmed "Marxist-Leninist" (communist), that he had been one since his university days, and that he would continue to "be a Marxist-Leninist until the last days of my life."

Cuba's ties with the Soviet Union expanded. The Soviets, now Cuba's main trading partner, also began to supply the Caribbean nation with massive economic and military aid. Raúl Castro visited Soviet Premier Nikita Khrushchev in July 1962; he returned with Khrushchev's promise to supply Cuba with increased defense weapons, including a number of medium- and long-range, nuclear-armed missiles.

Khrushchev knew that his position as Soviet leader would be in danger if he allowed the United States to dislodge Cuba's now openly socialist leader. He believed that, once Soviet missiles were securely based in Cuba, the United States would not risk triggering a nuclear war with another invasion.

Labels on photograph: MISSILE ERECTOR, CABLE, MISSILE SHELTER TENT, TRACKED PRIME MOVERS, OXIDIZER TANK TRAILERS, FUEL TANK TRAILERS

A U.S. Defense Department photograph, made in October 1962, reveals a Soviet missile site in Cuba. Soviet Premier Khrushchev claimed the missiles were intended solely for Cuba's self-defense, but the United States considered their installation a hostile act.

For his part, Castro accepted the missiles both because he did not want to offend the Russians, and because he thought the weapons — some of which had a range as high as 1,200 miles — would help Cuba defend itself.

The ensuing Cuban Missile Crisis — referred to by the Cubans as the *Crisis del Caribe* — was largely compressed into a period of six tense and suspenseful days. President Kennedy, who had received clear proof (from spy-plane photographs) of the missiles' existence a week earlier, made a television speech on Monday, October 22. He revealed the "unacceptable" presence of the Soviet-supplied missiles in Cuba, and announced that the United States was setting up a "quarantine," or naval blockade, of Cuba to prevent further shipment of Soviet arms into the country. Sixteen destroyers were deployed to inspect and disable, if necessary, any Soviet ships en route to Cuba that were capable of carrying offensive weapons. Kennedy also demanded that the Soviets remove all the missiles that had already been assembled.

The day after Kennedy's address, Castro ordered a state of nationwide mobilization. *Revolución*'s headline read: "The Nation on a War Footing." Thousands of soldiers and militia men and women were sent to coastal defense stations; new volunteers, even the elderly, flocked to help the militia. Addressing the nation on television, Castro said, "This has happened simply because, up to now, all attempts by the United States to destroy our revolution have ended in failure. . . . What have we done? We have defended ourselves. That is all!"

Four days later, on October 26, Khrushchev agreed to remove the missiles if the United States pledged not to invade Cuba; the United States quickly accepted, and on October 28 Khrushchev announced that the missiles would be removed.

Castro had not been consulted by Khrushchev during negotiations, and he was furious when he learned of the Soviet capitulation. Che Guevara, who was with him at the time, said Castro swore, kicked the wall, and broke a mirror. Later, at a meet-

An American warship, the USS *Barry*, steams alongside the Soviet freighter *Anosov*, outbound from Cuba on November 10, 1962. Visible on the Russian vessel's deck are dismantled missiles, removed from Cuba following the end of the October 1962 Missile Crisis between the United States and the Soviet Union.

An American cartoon satirizes the predicament in which Castro found himself during the missile crisis. Khrushchev's agreement to withdraw the missiles from Cuba (which was made without Castro's knowledge) infuriated the Cuban leader. When he heard the news, he swore, kicked the wall, and broke a mirror.

ing at the university, he accused Khrushchev of having "no guts." The immediate response of most Cubans was that the Soviets had betrayed Castro and the revolution. A new song made the rounds: "Nikita, you little braggart — what one gives, one gives for keeps!" The opinion among many Third World nations was that revolutionary Cuba, instead of achieving independence, had merely traded masters.

The Cuban Missile Crisis was a turning point in the careers of each of the three leaders involved. Nikita Khrushchev faced serious opposition within the Kremlin for his handling of the crisis, and two years later was removed from office. John F. Kennedy's cool-headed leadership elicited widespread applause. Fidel Castro suffered no loss in popularity for his role in the crisis, but he was now alert to the dangers of becoming embroiled in international power politics.

8

Diplomacy and Sugar

The outcome of the missile crisis had severely strained Soviet-Cuban relations. Khrushchev's settling of the dispute without consulting Castro had infuriated the Cuban leader and increased his desire for independence in setting Cuba's foreign policy. In spite of strong Soviet disapproval, then, Castro began openly and actively supporting armed revolution in Latin America. He offered the Cuban revolution as a testament that a rebellion could succeed through guerrilla warfare in the countryside and sabotage in the cities.

In late 1964 Che Guevara, Castro's most trusted confidant, sharply criticized the pro-Soviet communist parties in Latin America, which had, he said, been dragging their feet in the revolutionary struggle. "We know the revolution will triumph in Latin America and the world," said Guevara, "but this does not mean that revolutionaries should sit on their doorsteps." In a speech before the United Nations General Assembly, Guevara pledged Cuba's support for liberation struggles in the Third World.

In early 1965 Cuba began sending material support to revolutionary movements in Venezuela and

EASTFOTO

Castro addresses the conference of Latin American economists and finance ministers that he hosted in Havana in August 1985. The delegates to the conference discussed one of the most explosive issues of the decade — the $360 billion owed by Latin American nations to European and North American financial institutions.

A heroic representation of free Cuba dominates the center of the western Cuban city of Matanzas. The broken chains symbolize the defeated Batista regime.

Argentina. In January 1966 Castro hosted the first Tricontinental Conference in Havana, which brought together a vast array of revolutionary movements from more than 70 countries. The Soviet Union had expected the important meeting to be dominated by traditional, orthodox communists. Castro, however, was regarded by the Latin American communists as an unqualified hero, and he was quickly recognized as their spokesman. The Russians were deeply distressed by Castro's pledge to throw Cuba's support behind any revolution in any part of the world. In keeping with the tradition of dedicating each year on the revolutionary calendar to a major goal of the revolution, Castro proclaimed 1966 to be the "Year of Revolutionary Solidarity."

In 1967 Castro dramatically revealed that Che Guevara had secretly left Cuba to lead an expedition in an undisclosed location in South America. Guevara's mission, it was later disclosed, was to establish a guerrilla training center in Bolivia. The center was to serve as a headquarters both for Bolivian rebels and for the forces that would ultimately direct revolutions throughout Latin America.

Isolated in Bolivia's remote and unfamiliar mountains, Guevara and his companions were betrayed to the Bolivian army by the same peasants they had hoped to "liberate." The Cuban revolutionaries were surrounded and captured by Bolivian soldiers. Guevara was shot by his captors. On October 18, 1967, Castro announced the death of his close friend, saying, "Rarely can one say of a man with greater justice, with greater accuracy, what we say of Che: that he was a pure example of revolutionary virtues . . . he was an extraordinary human being, a man of extraordinary sensitivity."

Castro declared 1968 the "Year of the Heroic Guerrilla" in Guevara's honor. His response to events in Czechoslovakia that year, however, stood in sharp contrast to his words. On August 20, 1968, Soviet troops invaded Czechoslovakia and crushed a reformist government that was seeking a measure of independence from the Soviet Union. Most countries in the nonaligned (committed neither to the

> *If they want to accuse us of desiring a revolution in all America, let them accuse us.*
> —FIDEL CASTRO

capitalist West nor to the communist East) Third World, and even a few communist countries, condemned the invasion. Castro was expected, especially by his own countrymen, to sympathize with the rebellious Czechs.

Surprising the world, however, Castro promptly announced his support for the brutal Soviet invasion. He had been faced with a bitter choice: denying his revolutionary principles or offending the nation whose assistance Cuba needed. He had elected the practical course rather than the idealistic one. His decision, however, deeply disappointed many of his admirers.

During the revolution's early years, Cuba's economic policy was overwhelmingly "anti-sugar." Castro was convinced that the root of Cuba's economic underdevelopment lay in the economy's concentration on sugar. This monoculture, or single-crop farming, had many disadvantages. Because almost all of the country's income came from its sugar exports, any drop in the world price for sugar automatically caused economic suffering in Cuba. Furthermore, since sugar is a seasonal crop, much of the nation's labor force was unemployed for many months each year. Dedication of the country's manpower and capital to sugar also limited development

Castro confers with Khrushchev and Soviet President Leonid Brezhnev (left; 1906–82) at a villa near Moscow in 1963. Castro and Khrushchev had mended their friendship after the missile crisis. "I have no doubt," Castro was to say in 1965, "that he was sympathetic toward the Cuban Revolution."

EASTFOTO

of industry, which meant that Cuba was dependent on outside sources for almost all of its manufactured goods. And with most of Cuba's farmland used for raising sugar, even food had to be imported.

The new revolutionary government had, therefore, decided to make a push both for industrialization and agricultural diversification. Unfortunately, however, too much was attempted too soon. Local managers of farm cooperatives — many with little or no farm experience — were made responsible for deciding which crops to plant; the results were often disastrous. Much land that was ideal for raising sugar was ploughed under and planted with other crops, while sugar was planted

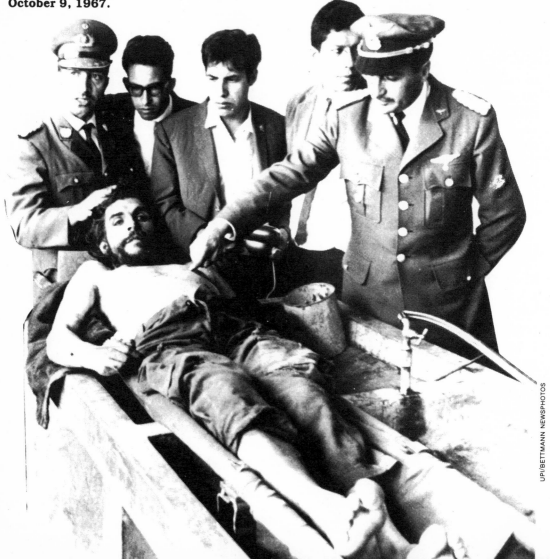

Bolivian military personnel display Che Guevara's body at a press conference on October 10, 1967. Guevara's attempt to start a revolution in Bolivia was an unmitigated disaster: he attracted few followers and was executed soon after his capture by Bolivian commandos on October 9, 1967.

EASTFOTO

in unsuitable areas. In the general confusion produced by the well-intentioned but hasty diversification program, fertilizers, insecticides, tools, and seed were often shipped to the wrong places, and even when crops were produced, the means to transport them to market were often unavailable. Not surprisingly, a sharp decline in Cuba's crop production followed the early efforts to reform agricultural patterns.

By 1964 Castro and other government officials responsible for farm affairs had decided to redirect their efforts toward the crop they knew best: sugar. The traditional Cuban approach toward farming — *por la libre*, or operating in a free manner, under which disorganization was sometimes seen as a virtue — was exchanged for a highly structured system. Specific goals for each cane field were set by a government planning agency. At the same time, Castro announced a new system of incentives for workers. It aimed at appealing to the workers' commitment to the revolution rather than to their desire for personal gain. Castro said that wages should be viewed as giving "a man participation in more collective wealth because he does his duty and produces more and creates for society."

President Castro takes a turn at bat during opening ceremonies of the 1966 National Amateur Baseball Series in Havana. Always enthusiastic about sports — baseball in particular — Castro had been named Cuba's best high school athlete in 1944.

The new sugar strategy ran into trouble right at the start. Except for the first year, 1965, targets for sugar production were never reached; indeed, the figures for 1966 and 1969 were lower than for pre-revolutionary harvests, let alone than for the standards set by the plan. Labor productivity dropped noticeably and absenteeism increased substantially. Workers with job security and guaranteed wages, it seemed, had little incentive to work harder or longer hours simply because of revolutionary appeals.

Castro drastically underestimated the difficulties in operating a complex planned economy. Bureaucratic red tape and a reliance on central decision-making created massive delays as local managers and officials were obliged to wait for instructions from Havana before acting. Gross errors in investments and projections became commonplace. One hundred expensive cane-cutting machines imported in 1965 from the Soviet Union, for example, had to be discarded because they were too fragile for Cuban conditions. New equipment and machinery would often lie idle for weeks because of the scarcity of qualified mechanics.

No area of the economy was immune from Castro's sudden personal intervention. The nation's leader was reluctant to delegate authority, and he insisted on managing even the most minute details at the local level. Countless decisions that depended directly on Castro had to be delayed for days or weeks while he was off making inspection visits. Fear of offending Castro inhibited critical thinking and initiative throughout the government.

Castro's insistence on maintaining direct control also led to some serious abuses of power. On one occasion, for example, the director of an experimental stockbreeding farm was experiencing supply problems. Feed had run dangerously low and the cattle were threatened with starvation. Because Castro could not be reached, the manager was forced to transport the herd to another nearby province. When Castro learned the cattle had been moved without his approval, he sent the manager to a prison work camp for six months. Exercising

Cuba will go on giving the African liberation movements the help they need, with or without the coordination of other countries.
—CARLOS RAFAEL RODRIGUEZ
Cuban vice-president,
speaking in February 1978

his personal authority, Castro made more than one irrational decision. Directing the construction of a major highway, for example, he insisted that it pass through, rather than go around, a rice field — despite the much higher cost — because, he said, "I want it to be possible to see rice on both sides of the road."

In 1969 Castro announced a bold new goal; a record-breaking, 10-million-ton sugar harvest in 1970. The harvest, he said, would become a "yardstick by which to judge the capability of the revolution." Clearly the drive involved a high risk of failure, but it was consistent with Castro's habit of taking on seemingly impossible tasks. Castro was playing for big stakes: economically, the 10-million-ton harvest would provide Cuba with much-needed foreign exchange earnings, thereby reducing its dependency on the Soviet Union; psychologically, it would restore popular faith in the revolution; politically, it would help revitalize Castro's popular support.

In February 1970 Castro said, "We won't accept a pound less than 10 million tons . . . it would be incredibly humiliating if we were to produce anything less than 10 million tons." The full strength of the nation's economic resources was placed behind the effort, and the entire population was urged to help. The public was bombarded with government propaganda. "Every worker should feel like a

Cuban peasants gather cut cane at a sugar plantation in December 1969. Hoping to reduce Cuba's staggering foreign debt, Castro called for a record-breaking 10-million-ton sugar harvest in 1970. Despite the strenuous efforts of the nation's work force, however, the 1970 harvest totaled only 8.5 million tons.

soldier in a trench with a rifle in his hand," said one official message. Radio, television, and street posters insistently asked, "What are YOU doing toward the 10 million?" More than a million workers from other sectors of the economy, along with 100,000 army members, were assigned to the sugar industry.

The final outcome — 8.5 million tons — was an all-time record, but it fell short of the goal. The costs to the economy were staggering; funds and personnel diverted to the sugar industry caused production to plummet in most other sectors of the economy. It was a hard lesson in what could — and could not — be accomplished with Cuba's resources.

Soviet-Cuban relations improved considerably in the 1970s: in 1972, the Soviet Union deferred payment of Cuba's debt until the 1990s and agreed to supply massive new credits for machinery, oil, and food imports.

Some subtle changes in the foreign area reflected the new rapprochement with the Soviets. Castro stopped his verbal attacks on the pro-Soviet communist parties in Latin America and retreated from his avid endorsement of armed struggle in the hemisphere. He began to concentrate on the development of normal relations with governments throughout the region. New diplomatic relations were established with Argentina, Colombia, Peru, and Venezuela, as well as with a number of Caribbean countries. In 1975 the Organization of American States reaccepted Cuba as a member. The United States continued its trade embargo, but

A Soviet technician (right) confers with a Cuban engineer at a Soviet-built power station in Santiago. As relations between Cuba and the Soviet Union improved during the 1970s, Soviet assistance to Cuba increased substantially.

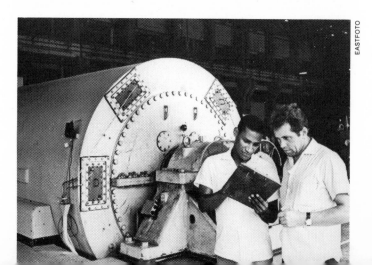

EASTFOTO

Cuba was nevertheless emerging from its political isolation.

In spite of this new orientation, Castro continued to aid revolutionary movements throughout the world. In October 1975 he sent some 15,000 soldiers to the African nation of Angola. The Cubans fought alongside the Soviet-backed government, which was battling two groups supported by the United States and South Africa. Although the Angolan conflict was still being waged a decade later, the Cubans were instrumental in helping the Russians keep the government in power. "If we had not made that effort," Castro said, "it is most likely that South Africa would have taken over Angola." Castro compared Cuban support to the assistance the French gave America in its independence struggle against the British. More Cuban troops were sent to Africa in 1977, when they joined Soviet forces to help the Ethiopian government put down a secessionist uprising.

The Cuban revolution became a model to Third World revolutionaries. In the Nicaraguan revolution of 1979, for example, many policies and programs of the Cuban revolution were consciously emulated; indeed, Nicaragua's revolutionary Sandinista government called itself "the second free territory in the Americas." Castro visited Managua, Nicaragua's

Castro, never able to resist a microphone, joins folk singers performing in his honor during a 1971 visit to Chile. The Cuban leader's host was Chile's President Salvador Allende Gossens (1908–73), the world's first democratically elected Marxist head of state. Allende died during the U.S.-backed military coup that toppled his regime in 1973.

Castro and Nicaraguan President Daniel Ortega (b. 1945) salute troops during ceremonies welcoming the Cuban leader to Managua on July 14, 1980. Castro was visiting the Nicaraguan capital to help celebrate the first anniversary of the overthrow of Nicaraguan dictator Anastasio Somoza (1925–80).

capital, on the first anniversary of the Nicaraguan revolution. Addressing a cheering audience of half a million people, he recalled that Nicaragua's deposed dictator, Anastasio Somoza, had asked the Bay of Pigs invaders to bring back a few hairs from his beard. "I decided," said Castro with a grin, "to bring back the entire beard instead!"

Castro's stature as a spokesman for Third World interests steadily increased. He served as president of the Movement of Nonaligned Countries (an organization of almost every Third World nation), and in August 1985 he hosted a hemisphere-wide conference on the debt crisis facing Latin American countries. In his opening remarks to the gathering, Castro said he hoped for "the broadest, most pluralistic meeting in the history of Latin America." Former presidents and prime ministers, clergymen, labor leaders, and the Nobel prizewinning peace activist from Argentina, Adolfo Pérez Esquivel, were among those attending. A surprise guest was publisher Miguel Capriles, a Venezuelan millionaire whose newspapers had long criticized Castro and communism. "I would even go to hell or heaven," said Capriles, "to discuss the debt crisis."

By the mid-1980s half of the Third World debt, which had passed the $700 billion mark, was owed by Latin American countries. At the 1985 conference, Castro argued that this debt could not and should not be repaid. Much of the money involved, he said, had been lent to repressive dictatorships that used the funds for corrupt purposes rather than for the common good. "When the history of this period is written," said the Venezuelan Capriles, "it will come to be recognized that, while other countries wasted time, Fidel Castro brought 1,200 of us here to confront what may well be the greatest problem of our century."

Indian Prime Minister Indira Gandhi (left; 1917–84) flanks Castro at the 1983 meeting of the Movement of Nonaligned Countries in New Delhi, India. An ardent supporter of the movement, Castro said its object was "to change the present system of international relations, based as it is on injustice, inequality, and oppression."

9

Castro's Cuba

The Cuban revolution not only transformed the nation's political and economic structure, it changed the quality of lives, the attitudes of men and women toward each other and toward their country. The revolution had a profound effect on poverty, sickness, and illiteracy, and it altered the way Cubans viewed themselves and their world.

Prior to the revolution, children from poor families averaged only four years of school. Many rural areas had no schools, and half the nation's children received no education at all. Castro made education one of the revolution's highest priorities. In 1961, designated as the "Year of Education," a massive literacy campaign was initiated. More than 100,000 secondary-school pupils from towns and cities were sent to the countryside to teach the illiterate population. By the year's end, some 700,000 adults had been taught the rudiments of reading.

In the years following the revolution, thousands of new schools were constructed in rural areas, and a massive scholarship program was instituted to bring rural children to boarding schools in urban areas. The number of children enrolled in grade

UPI/BETTMANN NEWSPHOTOS

Armed with Soviet-made rifles, women members of Cuba's territorial militia march through Havana's Revolution Square on May Day, 1981. Ceremonies honoring communism are traditionally held on May 1.

In Timal, Nicaragua, in early 1985, Castro announces a $73.8 million aid package to bolster Nicaragua's beleaguered Sandinista regime. The Cuban leader said he was "fully convinced" that the Sandinistas would win their war against the "contras" — American-backed rebels trying to overthrow Nicaragua's government.

school doubled, and by 1985, there were three times as many teachers as in 1958. More than one-third of the population (3.5 million people) was enrolled in school, including nearly all children between the ages of 6 and 14. The illiteracy rate had dropped to four percent of the population.

Cuba made large gains in the fight against hunger, an ongoing problem in most Third World countries. Food supplies, however, continued to be scarce. Agricultural production declined after the revolution, and, because of the U.S. embargo, the large amount of food previously imported from the United States was no longer available. In order to help pay its overseas debts, Cuba began to export much of the food, such as beef and fruit, that it produced itself. As a result of these circumstances, food was strictly rationed in Cuba. Each family, however, was guaranteed a nutritionally adequate supply of essential food items. Malnutrition, widespread in Cuba before the revolution, was said to

A Cuban student receives dental treatment at a Havana clinic. After the Cuban Revolution, all citizens became eligible for free medical services. The nation's new public-health system dramatically reduced infant mortality and increased life expectancy.

EASTFOTO

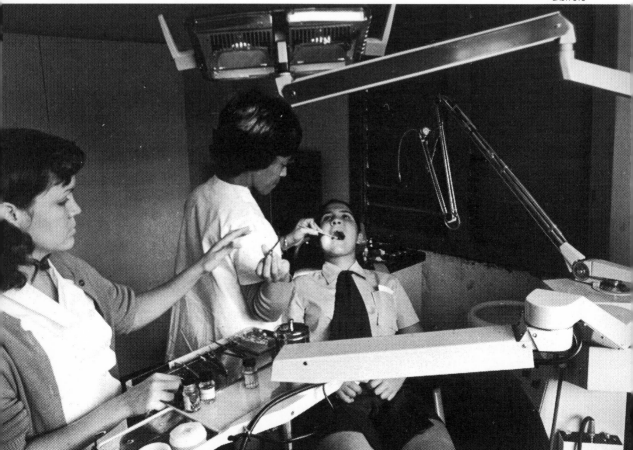

affect only three percent of the population in the 1980s.

The health of Cuba's citizens improved dramatically after the revolution. The nation's medical-school graduates were required to put in a period of service in the countryside. Major preventative programs and innoculation campaigns eliminated polio and sharply reduced typhoid fever and malaria; diseases typically associated with poverty, such as acute diarrhea and tuberculosis, were no longer among the leading causes of death. Life expectancy rose from 57 years in 1958 to 73.5 years in 1983, and there was a tremendous decline in infant deaths. The infant mortality rate in 1983 was 16.3 (per 1,000 births), which put Cuba on a par with most advanced countries (the figure was even lower than the rate for the black population in the United States, which was 18.1 in 1982).

After a history of slavery and racial discrimination, Cuba began to integrate blacks into all levels of society after the revolution. The status of women in Cuban society also underwent a vast change. In the prerevolutionary period, only 17 percent of the Cuban work force was composed of women; many worked as maids or prostitutes.

In the 1980s, women comprised 36 percent of the labor force. As Castro noted, however, many problems persisted: "Women still suffer from discrimination and inequality . . . we are still culturally backward [and] in the corners of our consciousness live on old habits out of the past." Most women continued to work in the traditional, lowest-paying sectors. Women's participation in Cuba's political world remained low: only 13 percent of the Communist party was composed of women, and few of the top government ministers were female.

The Communist party continued to dominate political life in Cuba. The party controlled all of the media, including the press, which had been censored since 1960. Cuba's crime rate dropped by 50 percent after the revolution, and Cubans arrested for ordinary crimes could expect fair treatment from the courts. Those charged with political offenses, however, could not. Habeas corpus (the right of the

Only oppression should fear the full exercise of freedom.
—JOSÉ MARTÍ
19th-century Cuban patriot

107

accused to be told of the charges against him) was suspended in 1959 and was not reinstated. Political detainees could be held indefinitely without trial. The Cuban government released no information about the number of political prisoners in its jails, but most observers in the 1980s believed they numbered in the thousands.

Cuba was not a police state (there was no systematic terror or torture of prisoners), but political dissent was kept within sharply defined limits. The lack of political freedom clearly ranked as the principal shortcoming of the Cuban revolution.

In power since 1959, by the mid-1980s Castro showed no indication that he planned to step down. "As long as I can be useful in this position or in another," he said, "and as long as it is a demand of the revolution, I have the duty to carry out my job."

By the 1980s, Castro was no longer the sole authority from whom all decisions flowed, but his personal power still was supreme: all the primary government agencies — the prime ministership, the armed forces, the ministry of the interior, the Institute for Agrarian Reform, the Communist party — were under his direct supervision.

Despite his power at home and his international prestige, by 1986 Castro had still been unable to reach an accommodation with his nation's closest neighbor, the United States. After the decisive break in 1961, diplomatic relations between the two countries remained strained. In 1975, testimony before the U.S. Senate Intelligence Committee revealed that between 1960 and 1965, the CIA had formulated several plots against Castro, each a mixture of absurdity and ingenuity. The American intelligence agency had considered recruiting Cuban-American gangsters to assassinate Castro, spraying his Havana broadcasting studio with a mind-altering chemical, poisoning his cigars, dusting his boots with a chemical that would cause his beard to fall out, and planting an explosive seashell in the area where he was known to scuba dive. Nothing came of these bizarre plans, but they left a deep legacy of resentment and suspicion in Fidel Castro.

Hostility between the United States and Cuba con-

Politics divides us, but humanity unites us.
—FIDEL CASTRO
speaking about
Cuban-American relations,
May 23, 1977

tinued in the 1970s. An antihijacking agreement was reached in 1973, but a slight thaw in 1975 under President Gerald Ford froze up again after Cuban troops were sent to Angola. Ford responded to the Cuban intervention in Angola by calling Castro an "international outlaw." President Jimmy Carter, who took office in 1977, lifted some travel restrictions between the United States and Cuba and expanded American diplomatic representation in Havana. This improvement in relations between the two countries however, was also short-lived. In April 1980 Castro permitted about 100,000 Cubans to sail to Florida in a fleet of small boats. U.S. officials were aghast when they discovered that among the "boat people" were thousands of criminals and mental patients, whom Castro had deliberately allowed to emigrate to the United States.

U.S.-Cuban relations deteriorated even further during the presidency of Ronald Reagan. Reagan accused Castro, whom he had characterized as a "ruthless dictator," of supporting revolution

Schoolchildren in a rural district of Cuba. Following the theory of Cuban patriot José Martí, the nation's post-revolutionary schools offered both academic theory and agricultural practice. "The pen should be used in the afternoon," Martí wrote, "but the hoe in the morning."

throughout Latin America. The Reagan administration reestablished prohibitions on travel, making it illegal for Americans to visit Cuba. In 1985 it inaugurated *Radio Martí* (named for Cuban revolutionary hero José Martí), a high-powered, Miami-based station beaming political news, soap operas, and popular music into Cuba. Infuriated by the intrusive station, Castro withdrew his agreement to accept the return of 2,700 of the "boat people" who were considered "undesirable" by the United States and who were being held in U.S. detention centers.

The refusal of the United States to seek friendly relations with Cuba was regarded by some observers as inconsistent, particularly in view of the reasonably cordial relations existing between the United States and other communist nations. Castro, however, indicated optimism in the 1980s about the possibility of improved U.S.-Cuban relations. "Sooner or later," he said, "economic and political relations will have to develop between Cuba and the United States. This is dictated by geography, history, and the interests of both countries . . . we are neighbors. We cannot move, nor can the United States."

A Cuban emigré in Florida weeps as she recognizes her brother among a group of incoming Cuban refugees in May 1980. Tension between the United States and Cuba was intensified by Castro's 1980 decision to allow 100,000 Cubans — many of them recently released from prisons and mental hospitals — to emigrate to the United States.

AP/WIDE WORLD PHOTOS

A jubilant, flag-waving Havana crowd celebrates the 29th anniversary of the Cuban Revolution. The nation's annual 26th of July holiday commemorates Castro's 1953 attack on the Moncada barracks, symbolic start of the revolution.

Further Reading

Bonachea, Ramón. *The Cuban Insurrection*. New Brunswick: Transaction Books, 1974.

Griffiths, John. *Cuba: The Second Decade*. New York: Writers and Readers, 1981.

Guevara, Che. *Reminiscences of the Cuban Revolutionary War*. New York: Grove Press, 1968.

Halperin, Maurice. *The Rise and Decline of Fidel Castro*. Berkeley: University of California Press, 1972.

——. *The Taming of Fidel*. Berkeley: University of California Press, 1981.

Karol, K. S. *Guerrillas in Power*. New York: Hill & Wang, 1970.

Lockwood, Lee. *Castro's Cuba, Cuba's Fidel*. New York: Random House, 1969.

Matthews, Herbert. *Fidel Castro*. New York: Simon & Schuster, 1969.

Thomas, Hugh. *The Cuban Revolution*. New York: Harper & Row, 1977.

Chronology

Aug. 13, 1926	Born Fidel Castro Ruz, near Birán, Cuba
1945–50	Attends the University of Havana; graduates with law degree
1952	Former President Fulgencio Batista overthrows Cuba's civilian government
July 26, 1953	Castro leads rebel attack on military garrison at Moncada, Cuba
1953–55	Captured and jailed by government forces
July 7, 1955	Goes to Mexico to organize invasion of Cuba
Dec. 2, 1956	Lands with rebels in Cuba; those who escape death or capture by government troops reunite in Sierra Maestra mountains
May 28, 1957	Rebels capture the El Uvero army garrison and seize a large quantity of arms
Dec. 31, 1958	Santa Clara falls to Che Guevara's rebel troops
Jan. 1959	Batista flees Cuba
	Castro enters Havana in triumph; appoints a provisional government
Feb. 1959	Takes office as prime minister
May 17, 1959	Nationalizes large tracts of farmland
1960	Nationalizes large private businesses, including U.S. oil companies
Oct. 13, 1960	U.S. President Eisenhower imposes trade embargo on Cuba
1961	United States severs diplomatic relations with Cuba
	Castro initiates massive literacy program during "Year of Education"
	Proclaims himself a communist
April 17, 1961	U.S.-backed Cuban counterrevolutionaries invade Cuba at the Bay of Pigs
Oct. 1962	United States compels withdrawal of Soviet missiles from Cuba
1965	Castro sends aid to revolutionary movements in Venezuela and Argentina
Jan. 1966	Hosts first Tricontinental Conference in Havana, revolutionary movements from over 70 countries are represented
Oct. 9, 1967	Che Guevara is executed in Bolivia while inciting a revolution
1970	Castro aims at a 10-million-ton sugar harvest; fails with devastating results to economy
Oct. 1975	Sends 15,000 Cuban troops to Angola to counter South Africa's attack on Angola's new communist government
April 1980	Allows 100,000 Cubans, thousands of them criminals and mental patients, to emigrate to the United States
Aug. 1985	Hosts a conference on the international debt crisis

Index

John J. Vail is an Instructor in Political Science at Rutgers University, where he is currently a Ph.D. candidate. He received his B.A. from the University of Chicago. He has been a community activist in Chicago, San Francisco, and New York City, and has worked and studied in several Central American and Caribbean countries, including Cuba.

Arthur M. Schlesinger, jr., taught history at Harvard for many years and is currently Albert Schweitzer Professor of the Humanities at City University of New York. He is the author of numerous highly praised works in American history and has twice been awarded the Pulitzer Prize. He served in the White House as special assistant to Presidents Kennedy and Johnson.